Poetᵣy 4 Grenfell

Voices From Da Grove & Latimer

Compiled & edited by

Princess Emmanuelle

Kamitan Arts

Kamitanarts.com

First published by Kamitan Arts in 2018
This second edition, published in 2019

© Kamitan Arts

ISBN: 978-1-5272-3541-0

Front cover: Image by Igor Barcleos for Kamitan Arts,
designed and edited by Shirine Osseiran
Back cover: Image by Kamitan Arts

* Kamitan Arts CIC is a Non-Profit Community Company. Our objectives are to explore cultural identity and the heritage of our diverse community, as well as highlighting injustices and empowering women. We do this by promoting community cohesion and understanding of humanitarian issues through the performing arts. This includes workshops and productions in rap-poetry, dance, drama, music, and film. Kamitan Arts works with many artists and youth practitioners from Kensington and Chelsea and beyond, thus we are well connected with the local voluntary and community sector. Our work has also taken us to Brazil, Egypt, Europe and Sudan, as we continue to develop and implement cross-disciplinary arts and cultural projects, which connect people, build and empower communities and helps create social change.

Live-ication

You Will Never Be Forgotten

Nunca será olvidado

Minigīzēmi âneresachum

Mesh hanensakom abadaan

Nunca vais será esquecido

Kaore koutou e wareware

مش هنسساكم أبداً

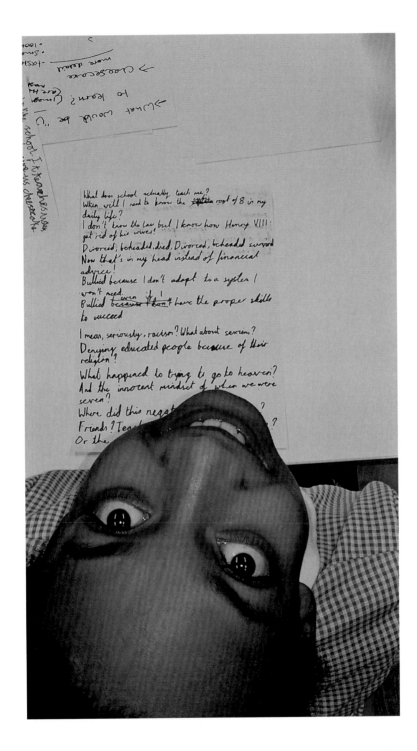

Contents

Foreword

Greetings to all,

I vividly recall watching the Grenfell fire tragedy unfold on a news channel that fateful night and what struck me the most was how unreal it all seemed. The first thought that came into my mind was that this cannot be happening in 21st century London; the capital city of a first world country with an infrastructure that is said to be the envy on many other nations. Yet watching the blaze intensify and being aghast at what seemed like an eternity, for anything that resembled the fire service to appear - apparently it was 6 minutes - was heart breaking. I have lived in a tower block before and became tearful as the thought of what those poor, unimaginably, frightened souls were experiencing entered my mind, wanting to look away from the screen whilst hoping, praying, for the blaze to be placed under control. This was a forlorn hope as the fire intensified and seemed to engulf the building in what seemed like mere moments; another thought came to me and as if reading my mind, a commentator stated, 'it's like watching the Towering Inferno'. That was the title of a critically acclaimed movie from 1974 that was based on a fire consuming a 'poorly constructed' building; they say, 'art imitates life' and perhaps in this instance life, tragically, imitates art.

72 souls perished as a consequence of that fateful night and accusations, recriminations and questions abound; who was to blame? Whose ultimate responsibility was it for the safety of the residents? What could have been done? What more could have been done? What lessons can be learned so that such a tragedy will never occur again? The answers no doubt will reveal themselves at some future point, but what should not be forgotten is the collective disdain and contempt that was shown to the residents, victims and the local community, premised upon their supposed race, ethnicity, cast and class, by those in positions of social, cultural and political power. For instance, the Prime Minister Theresa May has, in the lead up to the first anniversary of the tragedy, openly admitted that her response to the tragedy 'was not good enough'.

Writing in the Evening Standard Mrs May gave a withering assessment of her own performance following the fire. 'It was a tragedy unparalleled in recent history and, although many people did incredible work during and after the fire, it has long been clear that the initial response was not good enough,' she wrote. 'I include myself in that. 'The day after the disaster I made the first of a number of trips to the site, thanking the firefighters for their work and holding a short meeting with the team in charge of the response. 'What I did not do on that first visit, was meet the residents and survivors who had escaped the blaze. 'But the residents of Grenfell Tower needed to know that those in power recognised and understood their despair. 'And I will always regret that by not meeting them that day, it seemed as though I didn't care.' She added: 'That was never the case.' (https://www.standard.co.uk/news 11/6/18).

Now this grovelling apology seems to be sincere but I'm afraid that the pragmatist in me deems it otherwise; insincere, strategic, deflective, political...as it reminds me of, and directly speaks to, what happened in Southeast London, after the New Cross fire in 1981 where within the local community there was a feeling that the young black lives which had been lost did not have the same level of value as the lives of white teenagers. After the Queen and Margaret Thatcher (then Prime Minister) sent messages of condolence to families in Ireland when white teenagers died in a disco fire and said nothing about the New Cross deaths. This silence inspired a poem penned by Benjamin Zephaniah, 13 Dead, Nothing Said, which became a slogan for the justice campaign. (www.voice-online.co.uk 1.3.2017)

The crucial point here is the pursuit of 'justice' by ordinary people who, whilst having an investment in the political system, in myriad ways, are often treated as if they have no say at all. This was clearly the case after the New Cross fire and as a Lewisham borough resident at the time, and someone who knew many of the victims personally, I was compelled to be active and give support to the meetings etc. that culminated in the 1981 march. More importantly, it became a pivotal moment in British history as those who are generally disenfranchised and treated as second class citizens, displayed their disaffection in very public ways. This spoke to a refusal to be rendered invisible by those in power, which mirrors why the "Poetry 4 Grenfell - Voices from da Grove and Latimer", initiative is important to those who were directly impacted by the tragedy. The project, the brainchild of Princess Emmanuelle, a.k.a. EmpresS *1, of 'Kamitan Arts', therefore encapsulates the collective communal response to both tragedy and injustice, because her journey into spoken word began after a long-term dance injury. It was during the time of healing that she met Benjamin Zephaniah, amongst others, who encouraged her to use bilingual poetry to express her innermost concerns. This led to an opportunity to support various campaigns for social justice, including sharing her Word Sound n Power at some of his events, including opening one of his shows in her home town in Kemit (Egypt).

The above speaks to how and, more importantly, why the 'Voices From Da Grove & Latimer' project manifested during the emotional aftermath of the terrible Grenfell fire, that killed and injured many in North Kensington, June 17 2017. Its role is cathartic as the community needed to not only be supported from within, as well as without, it needed a way to heal through sharing personal narratives that spoke to the tragedy, the pain, the loss and the unnecessary suffering that was exacerbated by Government led indifference to the lived situation within that community. That is why the project is artistically eclectic as its sole purpose is to provide a voice for those who the State, far too often, render voiceless. Yet it is these voices that need to be heard and more importantly listened to, for they speak to the reality of a very preventable tragedy, in a multitude of languages and expressions that more accurately represent those most impacted on that tragic night and beyond. Consequently, the forms of expression that have led to the publication of this collection combine rap-poetry, dance and film, drawn form a series of workshops and performances, "all with the aim of alleviating the pain and giving a platform to the suppressed voices in our RBKC community since this horrendous Grenfell fire," Princess Emmanuelle.

I myself met Princess Emmanuelle at an event that was challenging social injustice, a few years ago, and was not in the least surprised to learn that she was spearheading this aspect of the community's response, to the way they were treated by those in positions of power. As such, her vision was to assist the local community in their endeavours to challenge the blatant injustices meted out to them in a practical fashion, in voices they own and control. I state this because, as stated above, whoever is in power, whichever party supposedly 'leads' the country, the one thing that history continues to teach those who are seen as less than full citizens, for whatever reason, is that disaffection and disenfranchisement is our lot and it is deliberate and destructive. For this reason, we must look to ourselves and our diverse communities to right certain wrongs and use our social, cultural, spiritual and political power to force them to hear our side of the story, for as Claudia Jones, who was extremely active in this community in her time, stated: "A people's art is the genesis of their freedom." The "Poetry 4 Grenfell - Voices from da Grove and Latimer" project is an exemplar of this standpoint.

Peace, Love and Blessings!

Dr William 'Lez' Henry
Associate Professor Criminology & Sociology
School of Law and Criminology
University of West London

Prologue

There is an evident disease attacking our come-unity for decades, hissing its way through our infamous Portobello Road and surrounding areas. It has recently and blatantly shown its veil lifted. The North and South divide as some call it, like we see in Egypt, Angola, Brazil, and in Dubai, is here on our doorsteps in the UK. This disease stems from a 'lack of love', as my good sister Harriet Gore from 'Touch Love Worldwide' calls it. It does not care about another, it is selfish and not selfless. This disease is Gentrification, the necessity of full Power and Wealth at the cost of others' wellbeing and livelihood. The need for greed can never be viewed as a good deed, and on the poor and weak it fuels and feeds. As we witness in faraway Rio we see right here in Portobello, Grove and Latimer.

Sound Records on Portobello Rd, where they used to sell my debut spoken word albums in the early 2000's - gone! Culture Shack where I used to buy my incense - gone! Acklam Adventure Playground and Play centre where I used to go as a child - gone! Westway Information Centre - gone! What was once called Subterrania and made its mark in our upbringing as the "place to be," with legends performing, where I also used to perform at an event called Dutch Pot run by local singer-song-writer, the British soul veteran Noel McKoy, - gone! Even the Ion Bar where we would perform with his weekly soul band - gone too! From Neighbourhood to Supper Club to Mode; Inn on the Green to Flyover to Westbank. The Westway Group with the North Kensington Amenity Trust was one day formed by and for the people of Ladbroke Grove, but now the capitalist agenda seems to have diminished most of the efforts that represented and benefited our local community. The 23 acres of land beneath the Westway was supposed to be community land. Yes, 'come-unity' land, for the people of Ladbroke Grove, not for Pret-a-Manger, commercial interests and privatisation. What has happened to all our youth centres and projects? LYC, YCTV, NKVDP, and even Wornington College, where I gained my access course to go uni? North Kensington library, my childhood local library is now in jeopardy as well as the Silchester Estate. The list is endless.

The council have been interested in selling Grenfell Tower to private investors for quite some time, with planning reports showing evidence of this. The funds spent on refurbishing it have been perceived by many as only preparing it for its fatal tragedy that occurred June '17, referred to as "Corporate Manslaughter". How could a faulty fridge wire cause the fire to blow up flames to all 24 floors and annihilate the whole of the Grenfell Tower block so quickly? Had the new cladding that was installed a few years earlier not been the cheaper flammable kind with combustible polyethylene core which released cyanide gas maybe the building would not have caught fire the way it did and the death toll not been so high? The residents had complained about the lack of fire safety, preventions, and obvious hazards years back. Should a landlord not ensure the tenants safety and do all they can to protect them from any failures? Who's to blame?

"They build luxury flats for the rich and build ovens for us," local filmmaker and activist Ishmahil Blagrove Jr stated while congregated at the monthly silent walk outside K & C Town Hall.

As I write this intro the public inquiry is well under way, with much scrutiny from the local community and public, much of which has not been given the platform to be voiced. Only recently have doors opened up to a few community members and residents to join the debate at the inquiry. It is a very difficult time for all the survivors, their families and loved ones and all that are bereaved. Many words, 'kalimaat', 'palabras' dominate my thoughts as I reflect on the 'Poetry 4 Grenfell' team and the many contributors with their lyrical offerings of expression throughout the year while collecting writings for this book. Words of sorrow and pain, words of anger, confusion, collective and inner strength, support, faith and love. We as a community have truly come together and stood strongly and powerfully at a time of dire need and despair; God bless our community and all its efforts, you can never tear us down! Some media researchers and reporters have been questioning whether we are now more dis-united a year on, even though we had initially all come together to immediately help those in need for 'Community Relief'. I told them I disagree, irrespective of our differences, once we have been called with a purpose so strong as this, we will keep at it together, until justice is served. Much respect due to all the grassroots movements, individuals and organisations that have responded to this catastrophe and call of despair, putting aside our indifferences and working towards a common aim, for 'united we stand, and divided we fall'.

I was raised on the top end of Lancaster Road, by All Saints Road, so technically Grenfell Tower is one direct straight walk for me; just the other end of Lancaster Road. I used to visit Grenfell Tower as a child, teenager, and young adult, all the way to the top floor to see my best friend and we used to spend some great times together, I can no longer do that, but what I can do is cherish all the beautiful memories in my heart and soul forever. This compilation book will commemorate and transmit our memories into written and oral living testimonies that will never be forgotten, giving a voice to the voiceless, without discriminating on ability, viewpoint, race, gender or language; this is for our come-unity by our come-unity, it is for everyone; everyone is welcomed; this is for YOU.

When I had decided to put a call out at the end of June 2017 for a multi-lingual compilation poetry book, which would include poems, raps, drawings and photos from my Grenfell effected community, I never realised the amount of love and response I would receive to my calling. During the months that followed the horrific Grenfell fire, we had managed to collect some truly precious heart-felt pieces written and drawn from children and elders alike, from 3 year olds to 77! Humanitarians, artists, sympathisers and activists in and beyond our immediate community have been given a platform to voice their opinions and share a message that has otherwise been manipulated or suppressed by the mainstream media. The Poetry 4 Grenfell workshops, local performances and Golden Trellick Tower award-winning guerrilla 'Best Art Film' at the Portobello Film Festival 2017, has given our community the platform to view, observe or chose to take part; using our poetical and artistic voices to vent the anger and pain from this awful tragedy and transform it into uplifting healing through the "Word Sound and Power".

All my life I had trained as a dancer, it was my number one passion and talent, yet my career as a professional Contemporary dancer came to a halt while I was at the Northern School of Contemporary Dance in Chapeltown Leeds. It was then that I embraced the Word, Sound, 'n Power, which acted as a healing tool when I was at a very low point in my life. I had crossed paths with notable Dub-Poet Michelle Scally-Clarke, prominent Rapper Black Samurai, and my creative mentor, the inspirational Dancer, Choreographer, Actress and artistic project leader, Ayo Eleanor Jones, whom all encouraged me to find an alternative way to express myself creatively. Also crossing paths on a few stages with the activist and well known and respected Dub-Poet Benjamin Zephaniah motivated me further to

18

express myself in this style of poetry as you will witness in my piece 'Anger'. It was at this moment in my life and career that I realised the therapeutic nature of writing poetry and the Spoken Word.

I had always believed that every voice and story should have the platform to be heard, recognised, shared, if the person wants to tell and share it. That we should be in control of our own narratives and not let the media shape it for us. The poetry created in this book has been inspired from and reflective of the voluntary writing workshops in our come-unity, the recitations and the 'Poetry 4 Grenfell' project as a whole, to help healing to take place and to amplify our voices of truth from the hearts of our distraught Ladbroke Grove and Latimer come-unity. I thank all those that have supported and encouraged my vision from the start including my community: brother Amon Saba (Karnak House), Amanda Beckles (GTCMP), Mike Medas, Joy, Neleswa - Community Relief, Shaun Clarke - Urban Word Collective for his on-going mentorship. Rebekah Raphael from One Love Grove for reminding me of myself and my purpose. I would also like to thank Jaqi Loye-Brown and Matt Trollope from Portobello Novella / MT Ink for helping me release this book to you in the time I felt ready to, and without claiming any ownership or wanting any financial gain, but encouraging me and allowing us the community to claim and represent our own work; just as it should be. Most importantly thank you to 'Rabena' (*'God' in Egyptian*), our Most High Creator for everything. My mother Amal, for being my number one inspirational Strong Soul Woman and of course to all my family, Baba, brothers, my habibi, and my Lion cub! You are all truly loved and appreciated, 'dua' (*'Thank you' in Metu Neter, Ancient Egyptian*)

'Live-icated' to all who are active in bringing solutions around the Grenfell fire and other such unforgivable incidents. May the souls of those that passed rest in divine peace and may the hearts of their families and loved ones be comforted eternally.

Let's immortalise our memories through the written and oral testimonies, for indeed these dear souls will never be forgotten....

Emmanuelle Marcel 'Ja' bbour a.k.a. Princess Emmanuelle
Founding Director and CEO of Kamitan Arts, Rap-Poetess,
Choreographer, Project Co-ordinator and Freelance Arts Facilitator
♀ ~ ❣ ~ ♀
Ankh-Wdja-Snb (*'Life-Prosperity-Health' in Metu Neter*)
Amen - Ashe'... ☥𓏏☥

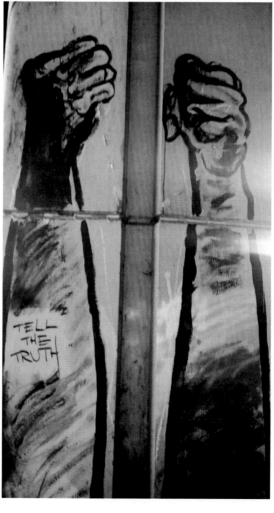

Marked 4 Life

Yinka Inniss-Charles aka Reason

As I look, as I look, as I look into their eyes,
So much deception those thoughts they can't hide,
Guilt which is masked by being scared to accept liabilty,
Whose fault was it really?
Now the whole world can see...
Was it greed or the fact of feeling superior to their needs,
The fact they devalued their lives, like an open knife,
So surreal,
Like a pack of cards they were dealt the raw deal,
So many broken hearts, So many tears shed,
That night when they went to bed, that night when they went to bed,
What thoughts did they have as they planned ahead,
Awoken to a nightmare which became real,
Yet feels So surreal, So surreal, So surreal,
No, No, No, Please Almighty don't let it be so,
So many tears ,so many years we will cry for you,
And while we cry we will survive!

Yet still no remorse just lies after lies, trying to twist up our minds,
They keep breaking us down, down, down
So many lives taken in one block,
Grenfell tower that last hour,
Those who saw, those who escaped,
I can't imagine what beholds their minds,
I can't sleep, I can't sleep it holds mine,
My pen in my hand but I can't write no more,
I hope justice is served, they can't die in vain,
Please let their souls RIP and Almighty please watch over those still alive,
those still in need.

Yinka a.k.a. Voice of Reason is a local old skool female rapper.

The Struggle Continues

Shaun Clarke aka Venomoustings

Black Samurai expressed in no uncertain way;
"THE STRUGGLE CONTINUES!"
In the name of truth and Justice, they said what they had to say,
As years passed by, the almost inevitable struck.
We took our eye off the ball,
Destined to fall, but wasn't it a preventable crook?
WE – because around the country, without precaution,
It could happen to many more.
Potentially, will it anymore, to those at risk,
who happen to be poor...
Who would choose such a destiny without question or scrutiny?
When through Unity, associated residents warned us,
tempted Mutiny.
Seems some are too desperate for a roof over their heads,
someplace to settle,
In a place where fore-Fathers and Mothers claimed the streets were
paved with gold metal.
Divided... we Gren-fell, and so the struggle continues....

Today, but hopefully not tomorrow, the struggle continues...
Unwavering, unanswered questions, authorised yet somehow
unapparent until too late.
Unchallenged when it mattered, when we could have predicted it,
without debate.
We paid our taxes to Con-men, at times elusive as the wind,
catching us out.
We went to sleep when we should have been awake,
We didn't imagine what was coming, that a common enemy would
give us a great shake.
And where was the mainstream media when some had spoken out?
Where were the professionals when dodgy plans were in doubt?
Why were they employed if not to do their work?
Looking the part, convincing us, in their tie and shirt.

Under the carpet leaving deadline dirt,
For a select demographic to be hurt,
A ticking time bomb, bound to explode,
A messy affair, set to erode, and then implode.
A festering nonsense that seemed fine at the time,
We trusted without sufficient complaint,
While evil was at play, without restraint.
The idea of prevention gets a favourable mention
Yet we can be too busy attending our own convention!
As the struggle, it continues...

Directly or indirectly affected, victims should never suffer alone,
I speculate – there's dis-unity, or not quite enough unity to find the
strength to overcome.
Busy with own post truths, genuine disruptions and distraction,
With the latest craze, games, problems, drugs, and lack of more
effective interaction.
Struggles we accepted long ago, whereby some wouldn't moan
because after all, this is England, not war-torn Syria.
Why would anyone choose such a predicament?
Why tolerant like we have no choice?
Why, like we have no voice?
Until it happens to us.
As we locate the oneness in our identities, that shared survival
instinct,
May we recognise and invest our power to change wisely.
Redecorate, contributing to a safer place for all,
Only by being culturally considerate, another way to compensate.
Doing something, beyond colour,
Looking out for each other,
As the struggle continues....

Rapper, poet, writer and central to the @LyricallyJustified urban poetry books.

Come Into My World

Princess Emmanuelle
*a.k.a. EmpresS *1* (الامبراطورة الاولي)

My World, Your World, Our World
My World, Your World, it's Our World

Come Into My World, Come Into My World of starvation, starvation
Come Into My World, Come Into My World of starvation, starvation

Mental manipulation
Chemical intoxication
Nature's exploitation
And the human's dem in deprivation
Govermental persuation
Through mass-media misinformation
Negative marketisation
And a 'unjustful' legislation

Come Into My World, Come Into My World of starvation, starvation
Come Into My World, Come Into My World of starvation, starvation

They give it intelligent fabrication
While they try and demolish our nation
Teach the yutz their own education
The wrong misguided information

Futile wars mankind's destruction
Greed 4 Power Speakin' Love Deception
Unjust killings disunited cultures
Hate and spite prejudice assumptions

Come Into My World, Come Into My World of starvation, starvation
Come Into My World, Come Into My World of starvation, starvation

24

We are a people of nations
We are a people of "One"
We the source of all power
And creation
We people are a blesSed "One"

We are a people of nations
We are a people of "One"
We the source of all power and creation
We people are a blesSed "One"

All we need is real 'livication'
To re-combine our falling nation
So there's no hatred or starvation
So we can peacefully live in Salvation

Come Into My World, Come Into My World of Salvation,
No more starvation!
Come Into My World, Come Into My World of Salvation,
No more starvation!

Come into My World
World World World ...

- Life-long local resident, International Rap-Poetess, Freelance Arts Practitioner
Taken from the "Born Into a Drowning World" debut Spoken Word Album.
This Word Sound 'n Power piece is influenced by Dub Poetry and Reggae, written
and performed in the early 2000's, yet very relevant in these days and times.
To 'live' instead of to 'die' in the word 'dedicate', influenced by Rastafarianism
principles and wordology.

From The Top Down

Jaqi Loye-Brown
(Portobello Novella)

The souls in the sky
From the top down
Every single one of you
From the top down
Forever in our thoughts
From the top down
We'll seek justice in the courts
Bring the top down

You done made your peaceful protest
To the top down
Used the process that was there
To the top down
No one listened to your plight
From the top down
About the safety failures there
From the top down

Rejected by those on high
From the top down
The risks were not meant to be your own
It was from the top down

A place to call your home
From the top down
A bell for every door
From the top down

Forcefully so cruelly snatched
From the top down

An hour after midnight
They were took down

No rescue plan perceived
From the top down
How a man threw himself out
From the top down
A baby thrown from where?

May God forgive us
From the top down

Believers and non-religious
Afraid.
Stayed.
Prayed.
From the top down

Local resident, Poet and published author.

Image by Jaqi Loye Brown (from a collection of urban cityscapes, 2013)

Corporate Manslaughter

Danjuma Bihari

Notting Hill, dressed up in economy cladding
Notting Hill - not the Notting Hill
Of Hugh Grant & Julia Roberts
It's its north face, the seedier end
Ladbroke Grove & Latimer Rd
The downslope of the seesaw
Seething with global humanity
The side slid down, back in time
To 1958 - remember that date?

The vested cannot bear comparison with 9/11
With the incinerators of Auschwitz
Tears may flow to the beating slow, of pan
Tears may flow; but stay your hand
Scimitars sheathed in scabbards
Surround-sound by a ring of steel
We beat our sabres into steel drums
Unrusting 400 years of un-dried tears
The tears of the lower orders in high rises
Are just so much water: "Cry me a river",
Go extinguish your own fire.
Your plight is undeserving of 'atrocity'
No flag will flutter at 1/ 2 mast
We will not pause the country in respectful silence
As for a stabbed policeman on London Bridge

This tragic tower of Babel, 4 decades old, 24 storeys strong
Pigeon loft taking prayers unto the heavens, where they belong
'Uz-kuru rabbakum.... uz-kuru rabbakum'*
Calling in a thousand different tongues
Licked by flames of improvidence and neglect

Charred corpses strewn about Ground Zero
Fledglings forced from the nest too soon
Property investors circumambulate: a diabolical dance macabre
Trampling baby bones & milk teeth
Invoking the final fate of Jericho.

And though it teeters, it stands
A colossal, upended, perforated coffin,
A recurrent nightmare, still-standing provocation
A leaning ruin of Pisa; the anti-Trellick Tower
A minaret defiant, still taking requests...
One lacerated finger in defiance
To the rich of the Royal Borough of K & C.
An effigy of Jo Cox, larger than life,
Arms outstretched above Rio
Smouldering, volatile J C
Turned into a pillar of ash
For looking back in empathy and indignation.

This is what a Holocaust looks like.
There, I said it: human sacrifice
Burnt offerings, the immolation of immigrants
You too, O grandchildren of the Notting Hill Riots
Now dispossessed of the Notting Hill Carnival
Watch Mr. Burns warm bloody, bejewelled fingers
Rupert MOLOCH, shape-shifting before the sacrificial pyre
In his offended nostrils, the odour of frankincense

The fragrance of corpses sanctified by the fast
Human sacrifice on the altar of corporate greed.

A baby, hurled from the 9th floor
In an act of maternal self-sacrifice
Her own unimaginable leap of faith:
Chief motif in a tableau of heart-wrenching impotence,
Will return one day in legend, on a wing and a prayer
Like Moses rescued from the river

Like an avenging Messiah
A smouldering ember; a brand from the fire
Will rise; a phoenix from the errant ashes
Reared amid the luxury of corporate divvied Endz....
.....Until then, the fire has been lit
Brimstone beneath the foundations
Of the Temple of Capital and its false profit.

Children grew to adulthood on that night
Voting, massing, turning heat into light
Sunrise, red sky, the following morn
The day of destruction beginning to dawn.

Poet.

*To the men, women, and children, martyrs all. The occupants of Grenfell Tower,
the living and the dead. The indomitable spirit of North Kensington. To all those
great-hearted people beyond,
who helped and continue to help in any way they can.
We owe our martyrs that much.
Urbi et orbi.***

** Remember your Lord - Arabic
**Dedicated to the city and to the Wold - Latin*

Un-Entitled

Amanda

You are the vista I will not ignore,
Your carcass still standing, strong to the core,
The strength of your heart made of all those you've housed,
The destruction you've suffered has us all roused,
For change, for a difference, uncovering more,
As the debris of heartache reveals what you saw,
What is this place we have always called home,
These are the streets we've grown up in and roam,
The cause is now different, you will not be forgotten,
People will see the so called 'down trodden',
Having a voice, this is no time for silence,
It's a time for the truth and not time for violence,
But there are so many who must take the blame,
Must give us answers, now we are the flame...
Of truth and of justice, of change and what is right,
No longer will we be a political oversight!

Local resident.

Nour .15

Words can't describe how im feeling
right now,
People say that it was an accident,
but ~~know~~ why or how?
I say we want answers and
we want them now !
Grenfell was a ~~tragedy we~~
tragedy we will never forge
A ~~tragedy~~ "mistake" the council shoul
always regret.

Di Grenfell Fire Ah Murder...

Lezlee Lyrix AKA Dr William 'Lez' Henry

Di Grenfell Fire ah murder...
Di Grenfell Fire ah murder...
Di Grenfell Fire ah murder...
Di Grenfell Fire ah murder...
What other word should I use, what other word should I choose,
When speaking to power in the face of preventable tragedy.
72 souls lost, those left behind pay the cost,
While they feed us with dross...to distract us.
Give them a 'special' day, just mek dem feel irie,
Spending millions and millions on a 'special' inquiry,
The purpose of which is to clear their name,
Apportioning blame, to hide their shame,
It's a callous game, but to them a game no less,
Cos the likes of us don't deserve the best...
Why?
To those who govern, our lives have no real value or purpose,
Electioneering in the community, when dem win they desert us,
Because we are mere political tools, political pawns,
Who they think they can appease with half-hearted reforms.
The truth is...
In their collective eyes our lives have no worth,
We are expendable, accidents, as a fact of our birth,
Reduced to an equation based on social position,
So being cost effective is an easy decision,
It's strictly business old boy, these are austere times,
More and more Government lies to hide their heinous crimes,
Cos if you equate the value of a product to the value of a life,

Then act indifferent to the struggles and strife,
You caused to the disenfranchised, the disaffected,
The socially excluded, the callously rejected,
Then in the court of life you're directly accountable,
The evidence against the Government is insurmountable,
Endorsed by public displays lacking in sympathy,
The leader of a country showing no empathy,
Fram mi born, Jah know, ah one ah di worst case mi ever heard ah,
Dat's why di Grenfell Fire ah murder...

Associate Professor Criminology & Sociology, School of
Law and Criminology, University of West London.

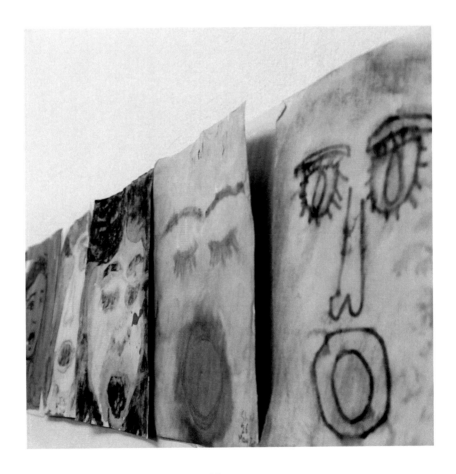

Unjust!

*EmpresS *1 a.k.a (الامبراطورة الاولي)*

Unjust laws
'n Unjustified killings
Unjust actions
4 Unjustified winnings
(x2)

Misplaced authority in control of the system,
Corrupting and confusing,
It's difficult to resist them.
If you do and are still outside, living and surviving,
count yourself blessed.
If you're not, then you're caught-up in the Matrix.
You're feeling emptiness,
hurtful complications to make things seem just,
but they're not,
They're just all wrong!
Twisted cover-ups,
are just all wrong!
Beautiful innocent lives being taken,
are just all wrong!

Just all wrong! Just all wrong!
4 the wealthy 2 overpower 4 long,
It's just all wrong!

Unjust laws
'n Unjustified killings
Unjust actions
4 Unjustified winnings
(x2)

Minority reports hidden,
from the public eye.

Equality now forbidden,
as long as the powerful few with control and authority are running tings.
The Beast is set loose,
to accumulate innocent lives put under unconscious abuse.
The Chosen Few, now chosen to lead,
take charge of their own destiny, and those of the weak.
Doing what we do best,
No doubts or regrets,
And no trust 'till we put you under test.

Unjust laws
'n Unjustified killings
Unjust actions
4 Unjustified winnings
(x2)

...'n just 4, 'n just 4,...
What is this 4 but taking the beast 'n using his flaws?
'n you hunger 4more?...

More corrupt laws,
Systematic underscores,
Underachievers, an excluded achiever of divine law.
-But u don't know divinity,
can't acknowledge ur iniquities,
den come tell me 'bout responsibility.
-U kiddin' me!

Unjust laws
'n Unjustified killings
Unjust actions
4 Unjustified winnings
(x2)

Life-long local resident, International Rap-Poetess, Freelance Arts Practitioner

This Word Sound 'n Power piece is influenced by Dub Poetry, Hip-Hop and Reggae,;
written and performed in the early 2000's with Black Samurai, yet very relevant in
these days and times. Taken from the "Born into a Droning World" debut Spoken
Word Album 2001, and Black Samurai's "The Sun Will Shine" Album.

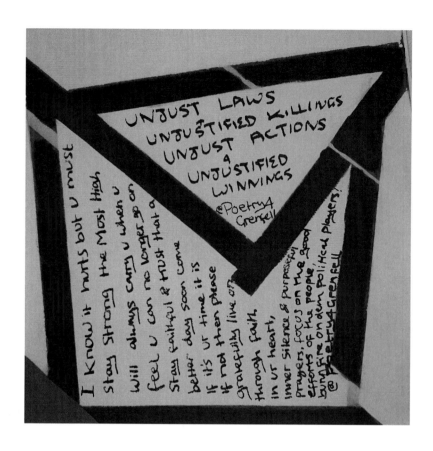

TOWER BLOCK FIRE: MISSING

Mya, 9

When I past Grenfell tower to go school I felt sad for all the people that lost there family and were affected. I could never amagin loosing my family or having to live on the streets. In latimer road there was lot's of poster of missing people there were people singing lot of events. People say it started from a fridge.

Grenfell

I ♥ Grenfell

What happend?

Little Madonna

Rachel Moidart a.k.a. Queen Shawty

*Get back to Shorty shortly and don't ignore the revolution at Hyde
Park Corner, Bringing together North Kensington
and the Occupy Movement,
Bring a drum, the all-night vigil has begun.
Don't forget to share, don't be square,
Be there if you dare,
We are ready to hijack the narrative with strategies of civil
disobedience. Passive resistance or obedience?
Do you want to give the Queen the blood money saved on cladding
and rehousing people now dead to renovate or wait...
For Judge Moore Bicks to divert the narrative with more politics
from the Inner Temple.
We don't want a riot. We want a revolution!
We don't want a riot. We want a revolution!*

E tu! Kia kaha nga toa! Kia mau te korero!

Stand up! Be strong warriors! Grasp what is spoken!

Ko tenei te huringa o nga hau!

This is the turning of the wind!

E rima nga hau e pupuhi ana ki te whakataka i te whakatakato i
whakatu nei i te Crowne.

*Five winds are blowing, the wind of revolution has come to take
down the system established by the crown.*

Ko te parimata i te kawanatanga. E taka! Kua mutu!

The parliament and the government. Fall! It is over!

Ko koutou nga Kaikohuru i tahu ai ra i nga tangata

You are the murderers who burnt those people.

Kua mate nga tamariki, kaore ratou e karanga atu inaiianei.

The children are dead. They won't cry out any more.

Kaore ratou e mohio ki toku ingoa.

They won't know my name.

Kua wareware au i nga tangata ora engari kei konei au i te po.

I have been forgotten by the living but I am here in darkness in the world of the dead.

Ko koutou nga Kaikohuru i tahu ai ra i nga tangata

41, local resident and activist. This poem is in Maori and English.

Ash Wednesday 2018

Andre Rostant

"I always buy The Big Issue in London
Because round our way, it's a load of Romanians.
I say you should look after your own first".
The ash-smudge as fresh on her forehead as a virgin,
Painted bride,
Sitting patiently on the old man's pyre
Before her henna has even dried.

"Of course they're not bleedin' rehoused!
They've all been offered stuff: mansions, penthouses.
But no, not good enough.
Stuff 'em!"
Away down the Ganges roll the remains of the virgin
And her formerly frail husband.

And I remember our mother wept bitterly
When we were slum-cleared from Vauxhall
Because she didn't want to move to Brixton
Or Clapham.
And I think of some moron then, sour as now,
Sneering: 'They should demolish the slums
With the scum in them.
Ungrateful spongers".
Smug with the ash-smudge of the faith of our fathers.
Not planning very well for their many-mansioned afterlife.
Ungrateful spongers, too?
I walked with a thousand people
In silence, in the cold, rainy night.
Past Holland Park,

Past many mansions here on Earth, and mews.
Past empty investments too.
Tonight, in silence.

And a bloke died just now in an underpass
Outside Parliament, in the cold, rainy night.

In silence, we walked...

Past the overfed and unconcerned;
Past the underfed and unconcerned
And all the detestable things
In this land of cheap, incendiary
White goods.

Calypsonian and member of Nostalgia Steelband.

Grenfell Indictment

Ras Makist

Ladbroke Grove west London imagine the scene,
It was June 14th 2017,
The most heinous crime of the century,
Builders filling their pockets while their hearts are empty,
It was human indifference not just error that caused the fire,
And it took nearly a year to even start to enquire,
Call it the crime that it is there should be
no pardon, that cladding?
The set up for the crime of arson,
Call a spade a spade let's take it further,
Forget corporate manslaughter,
The crime is mass murder,
Another part of the indictment is,
The poorer classes lost their lives on the whims of the rich,
To them its collateral damage, but to me it's sick!
So many lives lost for money and politics,
So to May, the T.M.O. And the powers that be,
On all of these charges I find you guilty.

A local resident and old skool rapper.

Justice For Grenfell

Zita Holbourne

So many lives that never needed to end
Trapped in a fire box, no way to defend
From the fury of flames spreading rapidly
Imagine how frightening this must be

They built ghettos in the sky to hide us away
Boxed in on top of each other without a say
Placed those who have children on the highest floors
No gardens to play so they're stuck indoors

Treated like inferior people
Never seeing us as relevant or equal
Disregarded then and disregarded now
Like its okay to treat us anyhow

Wrapped the tower up in a flammable cloak
Ignited in the night so the flames and smoke
Took lives, belongings & dreams for the future
What once was their home became their abuser

The residents warned of the dangers for years
Whilst those in charge didn't just ignore their fears
But threatened young women with legal action
Claiming their cries were an over-reaction

Now they with many others perished in the fire
Little chance to survive for those who were higher
Like the mother of a 7 month baby
Twenty four floors high descending to safety
But no way to escape, she couldn't get free
A whole life ahead for that tiny baby

Taken away because her life didn't matter
To those who ought to have cared and known better

Mothers, fathers, grandparents and babies died
Children and entire families tried
To escape from the flames before it was too late
Before they were assigned to a horrific fate

Many saved their families and neighbours
Some before that night may have been total strangers
Fire fighters couldn't stop the fire
Because of the cladding it spread higher

Some people were trapped for several hours
Calling from windows across to other towers
Even throwing their children to people below
Desperate to save their loved ones from the fire's glow

After. The humanity of communities
In stark contrast to that of the authorities
Whilst survivors find themselves homeless and displaced
Lack of action by government, complete disgrace

Failing to organise support on the ground
With devastation happening all around
People traumatised and searching for loved ones
Hoping help would come from someone - anyone

On the ground a floor of floral tributes grows
And on every surface the faces of those
Who died or are declared missing are smiling
At the memorial wall, we stand crying

Looking in sorrow at the beautiful faces
We hold each other tightly in warm embraces
While looming over us the burned out shell
Once full of the lives of those who used to dwell

Now a vertical mass coffin in the sky
Where forensic tests must identify
Too many who were unable to get away
And below a sense of disbelief and dismay

The cry for answers and justice rings in the air
And for those who have lost it's too much to bear
The pain and the anguish fills each day and night
Displaced, grieving, yet finding the strength to fight

While the authorities take donations away
The community is there every day
To bring those who survived love and support
But basic needs ought not need to be fought

Nobody who's been through what they have been through
Should have to navigate, search , ask for or queue
Or have to live, even temporarily
In a crowded box room, unnecessarily

Be orphaned, alone, grieving and homeless
While those who are negligent, seem not to careless
Ahead - years fighting for justice for everyone
What happened to them can never be undone

If it were not for the community
There's no knowing where they would be
And meanwhile a long battle for justice ensues
There's no justification and no excuse

What happened to residents of Grenfell Tower
Is the responsibility of those in power
None of us should rest until we see justice is served
And those responsible get what they deserve

Some try to say we shouldn't politicise
But if they stopped a moment to analyse

They'd see that everything about it is
If you're in any doubt just consider this

Seven years with the effects of austerity
More and more cuts without accountability
Add to that outsourcing and privatisation
Deepening injustice and discrimination

Security, safety and peace of mind
Shouldn't be things we have to seek and find
Working class people's lives are not lessons to be learned
We must never forget the night that Grenfell burned

Poet, writer, artist, activist, curator and co-founder / National Chair BARAC UK

"Art has the ability to heal and I hope that this book of poetry dedicated to all those impacted by the fire at Grenfell will be of comfort. My heart is with all of those who have lost loved ones, all who have lost their homes & with the wider community that have been impacted by these horrific events which were wholly avoidable. Justice must come and the truth must out . It is an honour to contribute to this book. Blessings be with all who read it & thanks to Princess Emmanuelle for making it a reality. May those who died rest in freedom."

Today I'm Wearing Green...

For Grenfell
Natalie 'Natural' Wright

A year ago today too many lost their lives
Husbands, Fathers, Brothers,
Sisters, Daughters, Wives,
Babies that had barely tasted life,
Those with promise;
Many living with strive;
The vulnerable, the strong, the old, the fail,
Lost their lives in the fire of Grenfell.

Green for is for go...
But they were told to stop!
To sit and wait
In that tower block.
While smoke grew thick,
Urged on by the flames,
Many sat and waited,
But no one came...

Next morning the shell was still ablaze,
Smoke still bellowing,
The acrid smell, the misty haze.
A community shocked; still in a daze
How could this happen? It cannot be!
This horror story ....can't be a reality!
The tales of trauma began to seep,
The haunted faces still plague my sleep.
The mother that let her baby drop;
Once she saw her baby was safe,

The fight in her stopped.
Hundreds shuffling down stairs; no lights...
Smog so thick; dark as a starless night...
Families separated in the commotion,
Hands torn apart in a human ocean.
No room to run
No air to breathe
Some stayed put....
Some tried to leave.
Desperate phone calls to those held dear,
Messages of goodbye...
Choked by smoke and tears.

The brave who selflessly ran back inside,
Knocking on doors; saving lives.
But as the time ticked on,
The smoke grew dark,
The flammable cladding was easily sparked;
Just as the residents had lobbied and warned!
But no one listened;
Their pleas were scorned!
Now look at the results of the officials' greed,
Children lost parents...
Parents lost their seed...
The fire set ablaze to family trees.
The frantic searches for loved one lost...
Hoping against hope...praying to God
Faces in pictures...shown from place to place
Still believing their worst fears would be erased.
But for too many the dread never ceased,
They were forced to face the nightmare
They still don't have peace...

A year ago I watch it unfold,
With disbelief... my blood ran cold.
11 dead? Is what we were told;
The media lie that the public were sold.

For we had waited and waited...
To welcome them in,
Laid out beds; again and again.
Created a refuge for the weary to rest,
But no one came...
So few were left.

Community hubs all did the same,
We did not know it was all in vain.
Rugby Portobello, Latimer; Westway,
Acklam Village Market, The Harrow Club,
Filled to rafters with community love.
Donations... Donations from far and wide,
The kindness and community spirit
Touched me inside.
We pulled together ...
We did what we could...
All races and creeds ...
Pulling together for the greater good.
Volunteers came...so many hands ,
Brother and sister helping their fellow man.
Giving their labour; their sweat, their tears,
Holding in the pain, the doubt and the fears.
We stacked and stored...sorted and packed,
Believing the victims would receive something back.
Mountains of donations...
Humanity displayed,
So much came, we had to turn people away.

But where was the council?
Not one official came,
No coordination!
Who is to blame?
The Royal Borough of K&C
Stood back and did nothing
What a travesty!
And our new Prime Minister Theresa May,

Stayed mute and disabled
For days and days.
I hope you're all haunted by ever a name!
I hope your heart stills burns
With dishonour and shame!
We won't stop reminding
Of the fate that 72 or more met,
Or the plight of the survivors
We will never forgot!

Justice for Grenfell!
We'll repeat this Chant!
We'll honour your memory!
Always in our thoughts!
Always in our hearts!

14th June 2018

My condolences to the families affected by Grenfell Tower fire, may you find peace and receive justice for your loved ones lost. To Latimer AP and all of the community centres and all those who donated and volunteered, I'll never forget the kindness, compassion and solidarity displayed, it was an honour to stand beside you.

#grenfell #justiceforgrenfell #nopeace #grenfell72 #greenforgrenfell #grenfelltowerfire

Let's Get Free!

Princess Emmanuelle

Freedom 4da mind 'n soul
Freedom 4da young 'n old
Freedom's not just a word of a story once told
It has existed b4 in Gold
So it must live on 'n be re-told
Habesha, Nubia, Kmt, Kush...
In da Spirit of Freedom I chant my poem...

Wat does it mean 2 be Free?
Free...
No restrictions
No Limitations
Da blessed opportunity
2 be Free

2 live Free
Without hesitations
Free 2 breathe
Free 2 drink
Free 2 eat
Free 2 think
Un-polluted and un-diluted
Un-injected and un-cloned un-infected
Good Health = Free 'n pure Life-force

Free...

Free 2 decide 4 oneself 'n one's people
2 be Free is 2 live...
2 be free
2 take from nature as long as one remembers 2 give
With respect not with resentment
Or regret-ment
2 be self-less
'n not self-ish

51

Free 2 grow 'n produce one's own crops
Not slave around 2 produce wat they strategically rob...
That's wat they call cash crops...
What's nature gotta' do with money?
Aint' it funny?
The way the beast decides 2 teef from our yutz tummy
They just a dum dummy...
Tryna profit from Satin's blood heavy money
Yammin' blood honey
Playin' crash dummies
With our lives
Most High spirit seed
Need 2 put things right...

C, Its painful 2 c,
I can't deny dis un-wanted feel...
Dat I feel...
When I c, hear, smell, 'n feel INJUSTICE around of me
It saddens and infuriates me
Angers yet motivates the Humanitarian in me
Allowing me to organise, protest and campaign,
Unite with like-minded, good-hearted souls
Trying to voice the truth of the injustice that we unitedly hold...

A perfectly planned in-house crime
Blamed on a mere electrical accident
After a fortune spent on refurbishment
In order to prevent such a tragic incident
And for years upon years the residents had complained,
Raised the high red risk flag
Outlined all the dangers and hazards that were supressed and ignored
Only to then face the horrendous disaster from 1st to 24th floor
I won't go into further detail
The repercussions have been intense enough
Yet thanks to our community's efforts that have re-filled each one of us
With soooo much Love

Striving to persist
Persisting to strive on

Never giving up
Hope or faith
That's what holds us up strong
Opening our hearts to accept the outpouring love from our come-unity
Coming together with soul-deep unity
Appreciating the efforts and long distant measures of compassion
After all the evil that has been inflicted upon our people
Focussing on the youth and their message,
Our future lays in their hands,
The new generation,
They be the blessing!

Our future lays in their hands,
The new generation,
They be the blessing!

Freedom 4da mind 'n soul
Freedom 4da young 'n old
Freedom's not just a word of a story once told
It has existed b4 in Gold
So it must live on 'n be re-told
Habesha, Nubia, Kmt, Kush...
In da Spirit of Freedom I chant my poem...

May all those Souls Rest in Divine Peace
Now existing in a better place surrounded by Love, Comfort and Ease

Life-long local resident, international rap-poetess, freelance arts practitioner.

Forever You'll Be Blessed

Alexander D Great

Grenfell tower's a tragedy, waiting for the world to see
And the warnings have been raised for many years.
People died in fearful flames – and we don't know all their names
But the whole community is now in tears.
Pray for mothers, pray for babies,
Pray for all - whose cries are in our ears.

(Chorus)
We never will forget you
You're part of our lives
We love you and respect you
Your memory survives
We pray that peace has found you
Your soul is now at rest
Our love is all around you
Forever you'll be blessed.

الحكاية في الدنيا دي
مفيش حد بيضحي
Why can't you see?
الغلابة بيتعذبوا و مش لاقيين
الي بيخافوا ربنا و مؤمنين
غيرهم بيبعزقوا فلوس شمال و يمين
مش هاممهم حد مبسوطين و مرتاحين
زي ما انتوا شايفين اهم عايشين
يا ناس يا هو دول مفتريين

حكم قتل و ظلم و عنصرية
خلاص مفيش تفاهم بس هيبوكراسية
انت هو انا ولا ولا ولا هي
يهودي مسيحي مسلم مش هي دي القضية
حكم قتل و ظلم و عنصرية
خلاص مفيش تفاهم بس هيبوكراسية
انت هو انا ولا ولا ولا هي
يهودي مسيحي مسلم مش هي دي القضية

55

Overlooked, not listened to – people just like me and you
Had alleged that safety standards were not met.
From the North, the South and East – we are mourning those deceased
But our sorrow's mixed with anger and regret.
Pray for loved ones, pray for strangers, pray for all
While all our eyes are wet.

Chorus

Local resident and old skool Calypsonian Singer Song-Writer (ADG 14-6-17).

This song was written straight after the fire. A collaboration flourished soon after
with EmpresS *1 a.k.a (الامبراطورة الاولي) and has been performed cosistently in
RBKC ever since; it is also the theme song for the award-winning short film
"Poetry 4 Grenfell", (Portobello Film Festival's Best Art Film 2017).

Translation of Egyptian-Arabic verse:

What's going on with the World today?
No-one is sacrificing why can't you see?
The oppressed are struggling and their needs are not being met, those that
fear God and believe. Others are throwing money left and right, not caring
about anyone-else, Just happy in their comfortable lifestyles; as you can see.
My people my people they are so selfish and heartless!
Wrong ruling, killings, injustice and prejudice, that's it there's no more need
for understanding! Just hypocrisy, towards you, him, me, or even her; Jewish,
Christian, or Muslim isn't even the issue...

Learn To Love Again

Maya Matanah

Looking all around the world
I see children crying...
Crying out for love
Seeing things that they shouldn't see...
Doing things negatively

And if we don't teach them in a positive way
They'll do what it takes to survive the day
Cause everybody feel the need to belong...
Even if the family love is from a gang.

The sad thing is... it's happening under our noses
The system knows ... this ain't no bed of roses
Some may say... you can be anything you want to be
But some people don't have the ability

Direction... Correction... Love... Not rejection
Direction... Correction... Love

We've got to make some time to love
We've got to take some time to serve...
To make a better place for the children of tomorrow...
We've got to LEARN TO LOVE AGAIN

Woman... you've got to spend some time with what you create
Man... take your responsibilities before it's too late
No more low profiling the values of the family
The children are watching... learning... can't you see?
Instant living... pack it in and let's begin again.

Make some time to love
Take some time to serve
To make a better place for the children of tomorrow
We've got to LEARN TO LOVE AGAIN.

Rastafarian songstress, spiritual/holistic practitioner and founder of
'Love Gift Vegan'. ©1995

Comfort In Knowing

Reg Meuross

There's comfort in knowing
That others care,
Complete strangers, people out there.
A weird kind of comfort when in your head
You're alone and your loved ones feared dead.

The cameras; the stares of the caring ones,
Or the ambulance watchers, press at the door.
Searching for snapshots, eyes burned with tears,
Hugs of compassion, child's shoes, charred fragments,
Black snow falling like hell's own confetti.
This marriage of grief and unsuitable pity.
A shotgun union bound by despair
And the hunger for some sense of humanity,
Some sense that we care.

There's comfort in knowing
Someone has your back,
But weird to see your pain turn to currency;
Look at these boxes of clothes, tins of food,
Gifts from the caring, the safe ones, the lucky ones
Turned out their cupboards, the backs of their larders.
Old beans, old pasta, old tea bags, old stew.

The town criers gather like flies, like hyenas,
"Can I lift this blanket? Can I touch your tears?
Is that grease on your face? Smoke and oil from the fire?
Don't wash it just yet. How bad do you feel?
How much do you feel?

How sad are you now? Whose fault is all this?
Do you have any wounds?
Where is your family? Have you lost someone?
Where are your kids?"

There's comfort in knowing, so why don't I know?
Yes, many have died, many are missing, lives unaccounted for.
Numbers don't tally...
But I see the eyes of the fighters descending;
The bloodshot despair beneath yellow helmets.
The tell-tale streaks on their young burdened faces,
The crouch in their back, the stoop in their knees,
The weight of the horrors they've witnessed,
The terror they've seen, the suffering.
The still, black unidentified heaps, the charred fragments,
The shattered dismembered shards of lives now gone.

Singer Song-writer.

En los Ojos

Yago Soto-André (YogiBeAr.E)

In your I's
Eye see mine.
In your arms
We hold the
Time
That gives birth to
Love that
Waters the flames
Into flowers.
I see in your eyes
The demise
But in between
The cries
I hear power,
Not death.
Love,
Not greed.
Life,
In play.
Yo juego pero
No.
No pude mas,
Y me quemaron
Los ojos por ello,
Mis queridos los
Arrancaron de su
BLOCK
Por sus cuentas de
Vajo costes
THEY FELL.
Pero volamos mas vajo
Mas alto llega el
Amor.

Me costo
Volver
Pero aqui me encuentro
En vuestras
Miradas
Me veo en vuestros ojos,
I see mySelf in your
Eyes
Beyond the lies,
Apareci en vivo
En los corazones de mis
Queridos y queridas.
And in our hearts
Our loved ones
Live on
Thriving on
Love
Not hate.
Not fear.
Let the hurt burn to
Ashes
And sprinkle the dust
Onto a canvas till
Our hearts
Bleed no more,
No more insulation
Around our pain,
More love outspoken
Plain,
n the arts of living,
Please
Rest in love and
Peace
Loved ones
And all in between.

Written in Spanish and English by a local resident, poet and activist.

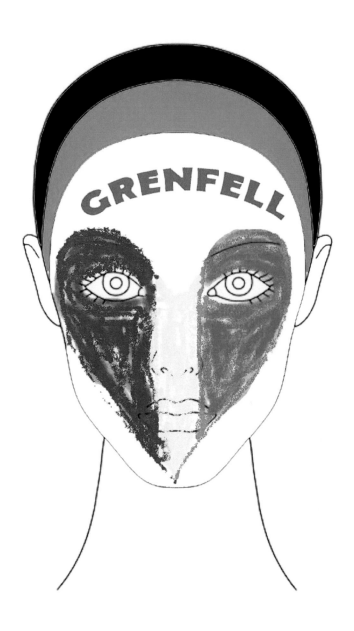

Endless Pursuit

Ruth Reubens

He will never leave or desert anyone
Even when his will is not done
He will pursuit us till our dying day
But we are free to turn him away
He gives us free will to chose his love
To be with him forever in heaven above
Or reject his gift and from him flee

Prominent local resident, rasied by Catholic nuns

Primeval Waters

Princess Emmanuelle

From Primeval Waters,
You Lost Sons and Daughters,
Take a Stand, give a help in hand,
Just like your Mama taught you.

Growing Vessels, Growing Seeds,
U Yutz of Adam and Eve,
Take a stand for the demand,
To protect our Breed.

This ain't the time to Divide
Time to Unite to Survive,
Drop the Ego that ur Feeding
Do what's right by these lost lives.

It ain't no competition
For senseless recognition,
Make a decision to help in which-ever way
you can upon this mission.
A good deed from pure intentions can go a very long way,
Ignore the jealous judgements
Believe ur heart and soul won't go astray.

No one has the right to point the finger
At your contributions, at ur intentions,
Do what you can, when you can
The ancestors appreciate ur efforts.

We are here with the purpose
to restore hope for all that's hurting,
Bring justice to our people
That have been targeted by this evil;
Greed, Power, Supremacy, is what we aim to defeat
Trust in the works of the Most High
And all your prayers he'll surely meet.

I know it hurts but you must stay strong,
The Most High will always carry you when you feel you can't go on.
Stay Faithful and Trust that a better day soon will come,
If it's your time it is,
If not then please Gratefully Live on...

Through Love and Faith in your Heart,
Through inner Silence and Purposeful Prayers,
Focus on the Good Efforts of the people,
Bunn fire on dem political players!

From Primeval Waters,
You Lost Sons and Daughters,
Take a Stand, give a help in hand,
Just like your Mama taught you
Growing Vessels, Growing Seeds,
U Yutz of Adam and Eve,
Take a stand for the demand,
To protect our Breed.

From Primeval Waters,

From
Primeval
Waters....

Life-long local resident, international rap-poetess, freelance arts practitioner.

The Longest Day

David Van-Cauter

I read in the Mirror
About the sun,
How heat rises through ancient rocks,
Creates a searing beam
And catches fire
On the longest, hottest day.

My skin is red,
Blistered from exposure,
Unprotected, fragile,
But you aim your lens
To steal my spirit.

From up on high
You deliver your news:
Your solution
A divine cleansing
Of furious flame,

And now the sky burns,
A beacon of ash
And silenced voices,

Sheets of blackened cladding
Floating to the earth
Like headlines

Published writer and tutor.

Uncomfortable Truths

Amy Guayo

Public cuts and austerity allowing the few a life of prosperity
Corporate domination and gentrification
Pushing communities into segregation
To greedy CEO bankers with no empathy
I shan't manifest no sympathy
Deviously tricking us into poverty whilst
your debt collectors are stashing up the properties
Corporations thieving water while slaves in Libya
are being slaughtered
And the UN overnight violating every human right
Corrupt politicians that for richness and for interest
Are prepared to wipe out whole nations from existence
Fabricating terror propaganda behind closed doors
Tricking the nation into believing this is a
war worth fighting for
We will rise up to your hypocrisy
We're not blind to see your policies are
systematically violating our democracy
While the papers are busy counting cricket scores
Countless bodies are daily being washed up
on the Mediterranean shores
Systematic neglect and managed decline left me questioning
How can we allow so many to be living on the breadline?
Thick black smoke makes it impossible to breath
Images so vivid make it hard to sleep
How can we carry on chasing our dreams when
justice is clearly nowhere to be seen?
Hereby I'm asking to those in power why every time
I see a high rise
I see another Grenfell tower?
If I use the word 'fire' should I feel uncomfortable

for my insensitivity?
If I smile should I be feeling guilty of passivity?
Grief eating flesh to the bone
Would this have ever happened if even half
in that tower had a different skin tone?
Corrupt political classes the smoke
won't cover your injustice
We won't stop fighting
Your fortress is fragmented

Founder of the Off Road Circus Project.

Anger

*Princess Emmanuelle a.k.a. EmpresS *1*

(الامبراطورة الاولي)

Anger Anger layz deep in my veins,
Anger Anger don't wanna b asleep again,
Da struggle's so deep,
I don't need to speak,
4 U 2 identify with da way that I feel...

Anger Anger Anger bwoy,
Anger Passion 'n Love 2show,
Anger and determination from strife I say,
Anger is just an expression and not a means 2 an end...

No solution stems from negativity,
Coz no hate comes from true positivity,
But when it's hard alone living in London city,
U wonder watz happened 2 da 'Equal Opportunity'...

Anger Anger layz deep in my veins,
Anger Anger don't wanna b asleep again,
Da struggle's so deep,
I don't need to speak,
4 U 2 identify with da way that I feel...

So itz not easy 2say that we're all happy,
Coz da truth of da matter, we're juz used or pitied,
It don't come a surprise, Police tellin' lies,
52 deaths a year in Custody...

As a proud Royal people we demand stability,
Start by deleting da false negative media imagery,
Juz coz we're talented no need 2 negatively exploit da screens,

Let's illuminate and respect our beautiful melanin...
Anger Anger layz deep in my veins,
Anger Anger don't wanna b asleep again,
Da struggle's so deep,
I don't need to speak,
4 U 2 identify with da way that I feel...

While some are living in excess luxury,
Over-feeding with their big bold money,
Let's take a look at da real reality,
An un-equal spread of wealth and natural re-sources...

All we want, is genuine respect,
-think that's what U call empathy?
Don't be coming 2us with your wrong ideologies,
We've clocked the cover ups that you think you do so well,
Filthy shame on all of you we demand JUSTICE FOR GRENFELL!

Anger Anger layz deep in my veins,
Anger Anger don't wanna b asleep again,
Da struggle's so deep,
I don't need to speak,
4 U 2 identify with da way that I feel...
Anger Anger layz deep in my veins,
Anger Anger don't wanna b asleep again,
Da struggle's so deep,
I don't need to speak,
4 U 2 identify with da way that I feel...

Life-long local resident, international rap-poetess, freelance arts practitioner.

Written in 2004, adapted in 2017

This Word Sound 'n Power piece is influenced by Dub Poetry and Reggae,
specifically Benjamin Zephaniah's; written and performed in the early 2000's,
yet very relevant in these days and times.

Its Beauty Lived Inside

Angela Harvey aka Poppy Seed

Grenfell tower brought forth a terror toxic yield
How could we have ever known its prophecy fulfilled?
How could we have ever known when Chelsea snobs bemoaned?
Its tepid tone inapt was needing to be clad
In robes of phony foam, fitting refurbished ads.
Danger warned and ignored, while overseers rubbed hands.
Its beauty lived inside, of fabrics stronger than pride
Of flesh not fire proof and so they burned alive.

Local resident, touring published Poetess, Creativity and Innovative coach.
Written in response to the Grenfell Tower fire tragedy 14 June 2017.
May those who passed over find rest. May those who survived find peace.

Murderation

Watusi87

"Out in the streets we call it... Muuuuuuuuuurder"

We also say don't trust the trust
Imagine trying to justify this mess in a few words
Still here I am unlike those whose bodies fell, stuck between a drop
and a harsh fate
Cry if you will, I wield a cry, tears not wet enough to put out the
what still burns at this day.

Oh Mothers, Mothers and Fatherless I'm ashamed how some of us
have used and abused Your name in vein, political and emotional
economic gain again. Who's to blame?
It seems theses steely members of authority have got palms of
blood,
They got it covered with mask and gloves, all that was necessary
for justice was hearts of Love, we ain't ripping off your doors,
gripping you with our claws and what more can you ask of us,
don't trust the trust.

You bore me with your news story
The real truth is too gory so all you got is new porkies what awaits
is overdue fury.
Enough fake apologies... conundrum, fake care, phony help, phony
philosophies for funding, Self fulfilling new born charities,
inconsiderate remarks and intellectual justifications Especially
when justice is vacant how can we trust in this nation, don't trust
the trust.

Spend a moment downtown
If Theresa May...that would be enough to turn Gordon Brown
The media's got it all wrong turning David's camera on

In a burning state......its Babylon
Acting the battles won but that's a con
We ain't spell bound on your magic wand and we still don't trust
the trust

There's people that survived still alive
We should have a weekly update on their lives, so we can see
what's really going on
I guess the celebrity range of pure elegance has more relevance
In flames goes your scientific experiment of negligence
Sorry mam I know your holding firm
But could refrain from escape and slowly burn
Because now is your noble turn
Don't worry by the time we found you
Justice wont surround you but......
Simon would organised a song about you
What a sad brave soul you proved to be compounded to the size of
ants
but we're laughing all the way to banks so thanks

Now it's time put Grenfell on the back burner
For a time we called it an earner

But out in the streets we still call it Muuuuuuuuuuuuuuurder

"Out in the streets we call it
Muuuuuuuuuuuurdaaaaaaaaaaaaaaaaaar"

Local resident, master words craftsman.

So What Simon

Mary Gardiner

Bridge Over Troubled Water
Is now an anthem for grief
For loss
For longing
But not for release.

Wrong anthem Simon, who said you could choose?
Paul Simon is good but not for the blues.

We need a Somali long song
A heart tearing poem
A medieval chant
A calypso or rap
And even all of them
Would not cut the crap!
Crying and sobbing and shouting
Cannot take away
Images of an inferno burning bodies alive.

Let this horrible, horrible event change all
Of the complacency that went before that night.
Let us look for justice and change and light
And never again cast anyone into the night.

This is not about mercy or grace or kindness
It is about justice and honesty and believing
We are all born equal and that is how we die
No amount of wealth can make us differ so much

That where we live becomes a rabbit hutch.
Change your minds you people with power
Or give it over and let us flower

In our area that we built with love
Something those with wealth have not enough of.

Look at us now, standing so strong, helping one another
And singing a song.
Take your mercy and kindness and stick it away
We need decent homes and we need them today!

I wrote these pieces after the fire.

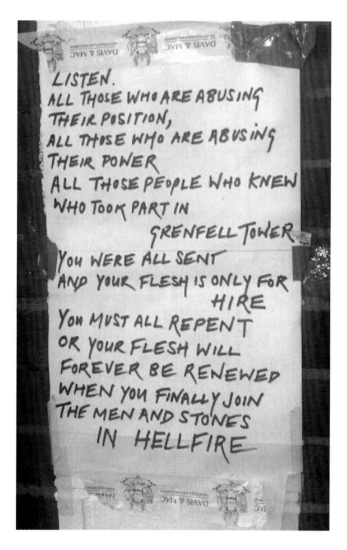

The Truth

Monera Takla

I wake early
The same childlike, blackbird tweets on the same branch of the
same tree
Next to me
Wild and free
Silence kills the soul
Silence lifts the soul
Reminds me of you and everyone else up there that day
Not knowing which way to run

Would you be making your tea now?
Having your shower?
Watering your flowers?
I see a lady your age wearing a scarf walking with her children
I look in her eyes
I see she is not you
Who is going to represent you now?
You have all gone
Amaya, you were three
Your beautiful, Arab eyes will haunt me forever
The child I would love to save
Give you a hug and catch you from the flames
To the disabled man, Hesham at the top
I wish we all could have saved you carried your wheelchair down
You had no choice but to stay
The young, the old
The brave, the bold, the young the old,
Every one of you
The young Syrian refugee
You came here to be free
You came here to be safe
We failed you here

Your last part of life
Full of fear
Yet, more a tear
We watch from here
You watch on T.V.
We watch here with our hearts and minds
The people who are left behind
How do you explain to a six year old girl that her friend has died in
a fire?
Too young for grief
Beggars belief
It came like a thief in the night
Some too weary and tired to put up a fight
Eyes half closed
Told to stay! Told to stay!
Faouzia, you would be here, be here,
If they gave you the chance to get away.
That night of blaze, blaze, blaze
Shall never be erased for me.

Give us the truth
Then we can try to set ourselves free
Their pleas, their pleas their pleas, from the tower
Tell the blind with all the power to give the people the truth
Tell them what they need to know
The people, the people, the people
We all have rights
We will put up a fight
Not all in anger in justice alone
We will all wait
The truth will all come out
Don't delay
The day will come for all
For now, we wait to release the cries, the cries from the tower.

39, Local resident. Origin is English Mother and Egyptian father, born and raised
in London. Lost my younger brother 21 last year, which inspired my poetry.

Echoes Of Dispair

Sabrina Smith

Tower standing so tall & proud
Tower home to many,
Many who shouted "save me!"
"Help! Help! Help!" echoed through the night.
As flames engulfed the building,
Within families, friends and single people....
With the hope of surviving.... the hope of staying alive.
It was just an ordinary night for many,
But for those in the tower is it was a frightful night,
A night filled with terror!
Oh how we wonder who has made the terrible error of saying stay
inside!
The instructions should have been run for your life!
Life so precious, life so amazing....
To have life is glorious and should NEVER be taken for granted!

Many perished in the tower that night,
And all it would have taken was a slight adjustment to the orders
given,
To save many lives!
As smoke engulfed the corridors and stairways those precious lives
were put on hold, for some live ceased to be...
Oh how I wish I had the key to unlock the mystery that is....
Why this tower, why did it burn so quickly, so abruptly, so fiercely!
Lives were shattered and taken.
Oh what an unpleasant and frightening sight it was to see how
they became no more.
Thinking of all those people told to stay indoors,
in hope of being rescued!
London will NEVER forget the fear that
gripped so many of us that night,

*Behind every door in the building, many people struggled to
breathe to survive, to keep their essence alive.*

*We must strive to prevent any such thing from occurring again!
Let's lend our minds, hearts, bodies, souls and wills to this cause!*

*Tower standing so tall, Tower standing so proud for us to all see.....
Grenfall was her name!*

*It's just such a shame she has been reduced to rubble....
Leaving the survivors with a troubled state of mind.
With kindness we can help them re-build their lives.
And, may all those whom perished REST IN PEACE ,
Let's make their lives count...*

*Take a stand and prevent this from happening again,
And please remember those who once were!!*

*8th February, 2018
A nearby resident, performing artist and model.*

Society Nurturing

Princess Emmanuelle

1 Path, with many passengers on the highway to the Truth…
Of Right Knowledge and Overstanding,
Peaceful and fierceful demanding,
Yearning, the striving, the burning,
-Mentally and emotionally,
For a once in a lifetime stability…
-Ability, to be, what you have the potential to really be.

Blood pouring innocence…
While others are scoring,
Betting, scheming, cheating on lives…
Mere numbers unjustly killed,
-IT'S RIFE!
…Hundreds, thousands and millions of ripped hearts, minds and soul,
Raped, tortured, sold and bought…
A heritage misled, you know the score.
And I wonder, I wonder with worries through the winds…
I wonder what will the weather next bring?…
More under-privileged, mis-educated, un-loved, under-nurtured,
Low self-esteemed innocent souls…
Could that really be what the future holds?
That turn to drugs, alcohol and eazy doe,
Or on the doll, couch –bums, always at home,
With no ambition, positive motivation or vision,

Just wishing…
Just wishing…
Just wishing…
That one day they'll know the meaning of…
A True Home
A Just World
A Loving All
A Society Nurturing The One 'Rabena' – Allah Most High Creator Soul
A True Home

A Just World
A Loving All
A Society Nurturing The 'Rabena' – Allah Most High Creator Soul

I sometimes wonder, do the instigators of such sin,
Ever realise that they could, never win,
Judging and controlling people's destinies,
Just wait and see what the Most High 'Rabena' has got planned for
thee...
For I am no judge, and I am no condemner,
I am just a Source of True Expression...
Through Right Knowledge, Thought, and Action,
I use the Word Sound Power to capture a fraction,
Of my feelings...
To share,

And help you feel, help you see,
Hope you feel and hope you see,
Pray to the Most High to make you feel and make you see...
For there is but 1 Creator for us all,
And s/he will always be watching me,
No matter what the weather may bring...
You can't hide from the Truth
'Cause the Truth is always watching YOU!
Said, You can't hide from the Truth
'Cause the Truth is always watching YOU!

A True Home
A Just World
A Loving All
A Society Nurturing The One 'Rabena' – Allah Most High Creator Soul
A True Home
A Just World
A Loving All
A Society Nurturing The One 'Rabena' – Allah Most High Creator Soul

- Life-long local resident, international rap-poetess, freelance arts practitioner
Written and performed in the early 2000's, yet very relevant in these days and
times.

*Rabena= Egyptian word for God

This Is Not About Hate

Stephen Steele

This is not about hate,
Let me reiterate... This is not about hate;
'Cause that's usually the first accusation out the gate.
When you have an opinion that differs from others,
So just take a minute and think about the mothers...
the brothers the sons,
The daughters and sisters the fathers,
Every one!
The lives that were lost, affected, destroyed,
Then tell me that you don't feel annoyed?
Tell me you truly think it's OK,
That it took our P.M. nearly three days,
To meet with the victims of this national tragedy,
Then she's bewildered when the country's #MadAtMay!
And what's with the lies, about the number that died?
Please stop trying to compartmentalise.
First it was 7, then 11, now 78,
But still over a hundred missing to date.
Does she think we are children who can't handle the truth,
That have to be protected on account of our youth?
Or is it more likely the P.M's running scared,
Because the U.K. is angry, we're getting prepared...
I mean just look at the people helping down on the ground,
And you'll see for yourself no elected officials can be found.
The residents themselves, they're the ones with the power,
To deal with the devastation of Grenfell Tower!
In the face of disaster, the people unite,
To try and fix lives, to fight the good fight.
But we all must stand firm and hold those accountable,
That only really care about the rich and the bountiful.
The people who think that poor lives don't matter,
Need to be shown they are wrong on the latter.
I tell you again, this is not about violence,
It's about a nation sick of sitting in silence.
While the government we elected to protect,

Sits back and does nothing but try to deflect.
I hear a lot about "clarity", about "strong and stable",
And I wonder who still buys into this fable?
But mark my words, the tables are turning,
It started the night Grenfell Tower was burning.
And it will continue right on up to the day,
That justice is done, do you hear us Ms May?
Until then I shout out to you all:

"HAVE YOUR SAY!"

Don't be afraid to enter the fray...
Metaphorically speaking of course,
Violence only makes a bad situation worse.
But use words as your weapons, the truth as your shield,
It's the only way these wounds can be healed.

I finish this now with a heartfelt farewell,
And a cry of justice for the dead of Grenfell...

35, father of three, barman.

Rich in Kindness

Monera Takla

Rich in kindness rich in blind
Tell them victory and justice are theirs soon
Tell them they need no silver spoon
Their time will come
Justice will be done

Living next to rich neighbours is not a prize
It is not going to cover up those desperate tears
and cries on their balconies
Their lives ended with burning choking smoke
whilst fleeing from an inferno
It does not cover the cries from the tower
the unborn babies yet to flower

It is not free to live there
Neither will it be without a care
There was no value on their lives

They had to die to get rehoused in decent homes
Yet some of you just moan
You don't want the victims living near you
What are they to do?
They need a home to call their own
You say you care
But where is your heart?
You want to show you care
You want to stop and stare
You say you work hard for your home
What of this life if you lost it all tomorrow?
Who would then listen if you were embroiled in sorrow?
How are you so sure what tomorrow will bring?
If you wake one night to a fire who will save you?
Your new Grenfell neighbours will knock on your door to get you out
Not a shred of doubt
Not a shred of doubt

Although their pots are empty
Their hearts are a plenty
They saved their neighbours
Dragging each other through scolding flames,
Through thick smoke that made them choke

Money cannot buy away their children's cries
Money cannot buy away the ones they said goodbye to
The ones they cry to
They had the clothes on their backs no earthly goods

Things are not as they should be
No luxury flat is free for them
Give them back their children
Take off the cladding
Give them back their friends
Give them it all back if you can
Put them back to how they should have been safe without a care
All you do is scream and complain
Put human beings to shame
You don't want them there without a care
Where is your shame?
You judge those
You lost nothing
Give them back their homes
They may have been poor but their hearts are rich in kindness
You are rich yes you are rich with blindness

39, Local resident, origin is English Mother and Egyptian father, born and raised
in London. Lost my younger brother, 21 last year, which inspired my poetry.

Our Wailing Wall: Ash Wednesday

Danjuma Bihari

On our Wailing Wall
Inscribed in low caste blood
Hieroglyphs of inexpressible anguish
Etchings of trauma and dismay
Symbols that still pulse and twitch
Runes of our times, of multi-lingual pain
Heartfelt scribbles, barely legible
Childish characters carved in distress
On our Wailing Wall.

Already a place of pilgrimage
We wander in sackcloth & ashes
Barefoot, impotent, breast exposed
Hearts calling till hoarse
Dead eyes, crestfallen, leaden feet
We lift our heads to the burnt-out building
Souls seem suspended, 24 storeys high
Pigeons, circling, nocturnal as owls
Bewildered, unable to land;
120 smouldering nests...

Below, on Ground Zero
A dog that lost her new-born litter
Spatters black milk on the pavement
Acrid with the stench of smoke
Love lacking an outflow
Ink holier than blood

On missives to unloved ones:
Unknown Migrants, Muslims & booty-callers
Remembered on our wailing wall
Amid teddies, candles, banks of flowers
Missives to martyrs & loved ones weep
Some supplicate, some contemplate
Some overcome, twice prostrate
Brushing the cinders from the tears
Eyebrows, false lashes streaked with ash

From Ground zero we rise, like always
We dust our foot soles and ourselves again
As we leave, reclaiming our shoes
Humbled, grateful, penitent... defiant
Foreheads forever marked
The date 14/06/17
Indelible, inscribed in Wednesday Ash
From the charred remains
Of all that remains
Of the names inscribed on the Wall.

Poet.

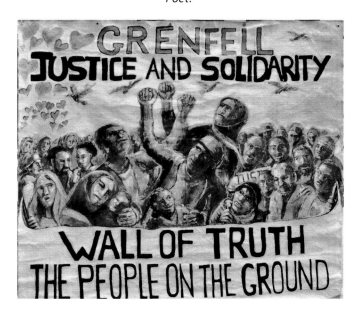

Inconstância Da Vida

Filomena Gomes Camacho

Depois de dor do parto ...
O bem-estar!
Depois do nascer...
O morrer!
Depois do prazer...
O tédio!

... da expectavia...
A indiferenca!
... do riso...
O pranto!
... da embriaguês...
A sobriedade!
... da estômago cheio...
A fome!
... do bem vestir...
A nudez!
... da tempestade...
A bonança!
... do eu...
A eternidade

Inconsistencies Of Life

After labour pains!
The well-being comes!
After being born...
Death awaits
After pleasure!
The boredom!

...From the expectation...
The indifference!
...From the smile...
Mourning!
...From drunkenness...
Sobriety!
From a full stomach...
Hunger strikes!
...From dressing well...
Nakedness...
After a storm...
Comes the bonanza!
...From me...
The eternity!

*Born in Angola, lived in Portugal, now resides in London.
Taken from Poemas Nossos (2009), translated from
Portuguese into English by Kat Johnson.*

Indifferent Britain
Without Punctuation

Ash Kotak

You chose not to see
the Lancaster West Estate
an island, a community
searching for hope in you
Presidential Labour leader
who waged war on their motherlands
these British people
worried about their own
far away
here too
as you fantasised
"democratise over there"
but chose not to see
that your land of hope and glory
was fighting the same wars
in Brenda's land

And in full view of you too
you chose not to see
you
indifferent future Brexit PM
who stood at your Royal K&C doorstep
human beings unlike you
not living in your million pound plus home
with your government of landlords
fighting for yourselves

You chose not to see
the 'others'

the migrants
the refugees
and the poor
in Grenfell Tower
caged
unwanted
in what was called
a multicultural zoo
neglected
unsupported
abandoned

You chose not to see
you
council leader
breaching all trust
boasting of your 300k surplus
panegyrised
at property developers'
black tie inductions
who hunted
Brutalist concrete gold
like a cruel blood sport
with the chilling calls of hunting horn
"shame about the tenants"

You chose not to see
the Grenfell Action Group
seeing sense
and reason
of an anticipated
precognition of disaster
without legal aid
due to monster austerity cuts
cutting away all equality
so they screamed out to you

private KCTMO
that's KC for Kensington and Chelsea
that's TM for tenant management
that's O for organisation
by fat cats
living in a parallel world

You chose not to see
you floppy mayor
with your abusive
"get stuffed"
inflammable cladding
under your watch
banned in the USA
and Germany
but okay in the UK

You chose not to see
fire rip to RIP
Melbourne's Docklands 2014
same cladding blamed
lessons not learnt
"but oh how nice the towers look"
where is the sense
where is the heart

You chose not to see
in a 10 million pound refit sprinklers
a fire alarm

fire doors
a second fire exit
why worry about health
and safety
when power's
aesthetic desires

control
your responsibility
your duty of care

You chose not to see
the people inside
suffering with
your failings
your callousness
your indifference
your neglect
your lack of empathy
forgotten Britains
gracefully
for their own dignity
standing up to your judgemental demand
of poverty disbandment
of class cleansing
of ethnic isolation
when you demand they move
from London to elsewhere
so you can forget
and ignore
social injustice

You chose not to see
the sharp toothed jaw
of diamond clustered gentrification
in the richest borough
in an international city
in the world's 5th economy

You chose not to see housing monster
under a new hard Brexit PM
when you sat on
an urgent
to the 'others'

fire safety review
about saving their lives
in their only home tower blocks
but why would you care
because they were not you

You chose not to see
now as Chief of Staff
the cold Prime-Monster
on her strong and stable
Britain exit drive
pretending her un-united UK
suddenly
stood still
whilst our Queen's people cried

You chose not to see
when
finally
prescience and reality
exploded
on the island
making world news
as Grenfell Tower burns
with
human beings
and their lives
their families

their histories
their memories
their hopes
their dreams....

You chose not to see
visiting PM TM

your betrayal of duty
by refusing
to speak
to hold
to hug
to kiss
those grieving,
broken,
stunned,
human beings
the same as you
still hearing the echoes of children's helpless
"help me,
help me"
standing at windows
ordered to stay trapped
in homes
by the council official signs
and the police

You chose not to see
that you all were having a laugh
at the expense of lives
beyond the burning rage
crying out to those below shaking
hopeless
outraged
hurting
"get out
get out"
Britain's historical problem that just won't go away
You chose not to see
communities cohesion

you can't
you won't
you don't want to

or is it you don't care to
when London
came together
no difference
united
as one

You chose not to see
the soaring spirits screaming from above
the dead searching for the living
the living holding hope
for the disappeared
praying together
all religions
all beliefs
united in grief
God and gods
Allah
Jesus Christ
Rama
Buddha
all the same to me

You chose not to see when you ordered
a government led enquiry
no independent inquest
denying

the "others"
a public voice
as the country grieves
for our own humanity
and our collective indifference
You choose not to see
what the UK can no longer ignore
yesterday

is can never again be today
nor a broken tomorrow
in our land
our home
where the poor
have lost all hope
and a black tower
stands
in defiance
an artistic reminder
of a criminal act

You choose not to see
the anger
the tears
the pain
crying
"hark Britain
rise up
take these damning images
stuck in your heads
as a symbol of disempowered
Britains
in an unequal
broken
1 plus 3 equals
a 4th world society

that self-congratulatory
Western
racist term"
You choose not to see
even after all is stripped raw
for the world to gasp
London 2017
Britain 2017

a conspiracy of austerity,
profiteering
democratic unaccountability
avarice
corruption
intimidation
coercion
of the most vulnerable
and marginalised
the voiceless
that's Grenfell Tower
so says word on the street
you will see
I wonder who made the big money
your Neo-liberalism experiment is discredited!

You choose not to see
the charcoaled dead
huddled together for strength
whole families
whole floors
seeing the full horror of their fate
making final phone calls
love over anger and hate
whilst waiting to die
asking

"how could this happen
why didn't anyone come
why the suffocating smoke

why the 1000 degree flames"
I hope many stayed asleep
I hope they find jannah
and heaven
close your eyes

sleep
goodbye
rest in peace
We are hear to fight for you.

© June 2017
Poet, filmmaker, arts facilitator.

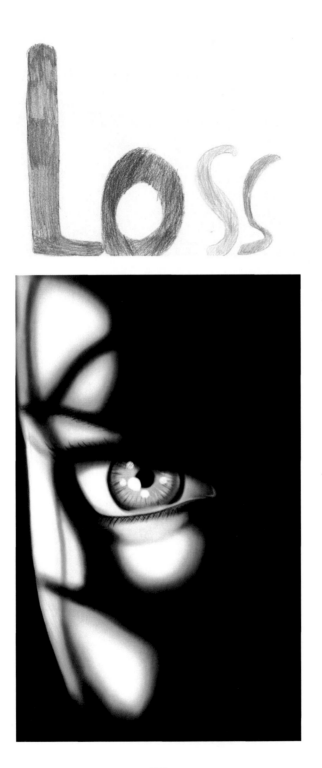

Underneath her Veil

Monera Takla

Underneath her veil
Underneath her veil
Is a devoted mother unlike any other
Underneath her veil
Is a true friend until the very end
Never one to pretend

Underneath her veil
Is a loyal wife
Is a student of life

Underneath her veil
Is an aunty, a future grandmother of three
Never meant to be

Underneath her veil
Is a caring, kind, decent, lady
An innocent, ageless face
That sees no more

From underneath her veil
She has gone.

18.6.17

39, Local resident, origin is English Mother and Egyptian father, born and raised in London. Lost my younger brother, 21 last year, which inspired my poetry.

Nothing

Rowan May Early Wray

Crying
Fear
Nothing

Pain
Hurt
Nothing

Sadness
Anger
Nothing

Neglect
Lost
Nothing

Confused
Unknowing
Nothing

Tragedy
Heartache
Nothing

Blood
Tears
Nothing..... Oblivion

Year 8 student at Morpeth School, East London.

Catastrophe

Andy Aldersley

(My heartfelt poem for the victims and families)

Catastrophe is not the word
Fire alarms could not be heard.
In Grenfell tower on that tragic night, the safety measures just
weren't right;
Fast asleep not really knowing,
That while they slept the flames were growing.
When they woke they began to choke,
Breathing in the thick black smoke.
Sirens wailed down below,
As the crowds began to grow.
Banging windows and shouting down,
Terrified people screamed so loud.
They had no option at this stage,
as the flames began to rage.
They were told to stay inside,
Families below could hear their cries.
Desperate families on their phones,
Final words and then their groans.
The brave fire service did all they could,
But the flames kept rising... too far above.
People shocked and felt so numb,
What the hell have the council done?!
The safety fears.... fell on deaf ears!!!
These poor people had complained for years and years;
Time and time they had been told...
That all this danger would unfold.
This ticking time bomb in the sky
Where generations were left to die.
Now it's too late, and lives are lost,

Please wake up now !!!
And count the cost!!!
Too many people on that tragic night,
Inhaled the smoke and lost their fight.
Kensington Town you should be proud,
Amazing people that have rallied around!
This heartfelt bond within your town,
Such wonderful people from all around.

Not forgotten-God bless to you.
Rest in peace to the seventy two

49, Dad from Bolton
I love to write poems and thought it was appropriate to
write this poem the day after this tragic event.

Grenfell Pyre

Catherine Henney

A charcoal finger skyward points
Disturbing us at it anoints
Accusing all of us
Of not acting soon enough
Yes we watched you waving yes
We watched you burnt down
Smoked out
We recoiled at shouts of help
I saw you at your window yesterday
Your younger daughter waved my way
Now I look right through
Your rough clad sarcophagus
Photo frames of each one of you
Could have been any one of us
Flowers spill up steps
As summers dusty evening air laments
A black haired boy
A brown eyed girl
Wrinkled bent backed men
Now we stand bent
Stooped digesting messages
Written by the living
Read by the grieving
Torturing the tears
From the sobbing bereaving
As green trees
Brashly flaunt their leaves
But some still lay in that tower block
Waiting for us to claim them
As voices still reverberate

Against the smoked out walls too late
We read notices and names on posts
Of living rich despicable ghosts
Rhetoric from these odious fools
Never learned about people in their affluent schools
Like arms the church door stands wide open
So many stop and linger hoping
For some acceptance
Something near to God
And here we are no faith but that we could
Love more each other
Sister brother
Lost souls last breaths
Once lives now deaths

Poet from Liverpool.

One Wednesday

Hayat Emilie Osseiran Pistecky

Not far away
On a gloomy Wednesday
A fire started and
Raced all the way
As fast as a cheetah
Catching its prey
It raced faster and faster
Until it faded away
So all the memories will forever stay
And never ever go away.

8 year old local resident.

My Will

Hesham Rahman

My Will, for who will remember me one day.
Remember my presence before my departure.
To see a smile on your face when I'm gone.
A prayer from your heart, no tears or sadness near my grave.
If we shared a memory that's in your heart, always remember it
with a smile, for who will remember me one day, remember my
presence before my departure.

Egyptian Grenfell resident RIP - written February 2016.

Fallen Hide Gone Heal

Brooke Traversari

Fallen
Fallen into ashes
Fallen with the tower
Fallen without a fight
Hide
Hide the reason
Hide with the smoke
Hide with the evidence
Gone
Gone like the girl who isn't coming back
Gone like the homes and lives
Gone like the towers' walls
Heal
Heal the families
Heal the injuries
Heal the wreckage
But how will we heal the nightmares?

Year 8 student at Morpeth School, East London.

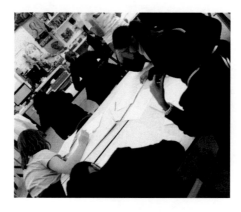

Grenfell is Empty

Christina Sealy

I woke up extra early that morning
The phones alarmed that Grenfell was on fire
I looked out of the back window with my family
At the two towers in our skyline
We saw a moving image that looked like one twin tower
With no aeroplanes
And no helicopters
Every single window
Was smothered in smoke
It was more than smoke
It was thoroughly full of pumping pallid poison
Pumping in gunmetal or battleship grey
Betraying the brutalist design of the 1967 era
Betraying the dead and destitute
Not stopping to overlook or underrepresent
At once screaming that hundreds had departed
Whilst also burning alive over 24 floors for 24 more hours
Both finished and far from finished
"No" I said
"The building has recently been refurbished
Everybody moved out
They haven't moved back in yet
Grenfell is empty"

Local resident, mother of Vienna, 5 and Carmen, 3.

In the Air

Monera Takla

The air is silent around Grenf
The blackbirds sing from the treetops on high
The air is stiffly silent
We hear the children's cries, cries.
Turn on the radio and t.v we hear lies, lies.

The people we loved and knew are in the air everywhere
We are keen to show we care, we care
We love them
We want justice for our friends mums, neighbours, dads, uncles
aunts, brothers, nans, grandads babies yet to come
These feelings can never be undone.

Their spirits live in the air
Everywhere
How we want to know the truth
Although it may never undo the damage that has been done
The truth is where will we go from here?
Yet full of fear
Too weary from shedding tears

We do care
We do care
Don't just stop and stare taking pictures
here and there without a care!
This isn't the place
Give the people their space, space.
Children we love, friends we love are resting there
Don't just walk without a care or just stop and stare
Think of the innocent souls we love who are way on high up above

in the tower.
Young lives still not yet in bloom
Left us all too soon, too soon
Their only crime, no silver spoon

Old and young gone before their time, time
For them the clock no longer chimes
Never, ever, ever let this happen again, again
The eyes, the eyes
The cries, the cries from the Grenfell tower
The unborn babies yet to flower
Only we have the power for change
To make the government re-arrange
Don't just turn the page

Don't try to gather in rage
Time for change
It is too late for them
This can never happen again.

The eyes, the eyes
The cries, the cries
The blame, the blame
The shame, the shame
This can never happen again...

Again.

*Being the voice of the helpless and vulnerable victims who were
in the tower and didn't survive, and those who did survive.
For friends, families and neighbours*

*39, Origin is English Mother and Egyptian father, born and raised in London.
Lost my younger brother 21 last year, which inspired my poetry.*

What Do These Words Mean?

Ayub Shariff

Ashes carried away by the hot summer breeze
Sprinkled all over the gardens
Maybe to show how death stems from life
Grenfell is at heart with many people
And how many hearts perished that day?
Children screaming
Not knowing the fruits of life
It was already fleeting
Imagine having to open your eyes only to lose them for the last
Tragedy
Loss
What do these words mean to us?
To me?

*Inspired by Monera Takla's 'Beside The Fallen Ashes', Year. 8
student at Morpeth School, East London.*

Black Block

Toby (Tee El Bee)

Black block
Silhouette of pain in the sky
Black block
Soaking up the rain as we cry
Black block
Reminding us of things we have lost
Black block
Showing us the struggle's real cost
Black block
Ash and debris blowing in the wind
Black block
Worry bout what we are breathing in
Black block
Children's dreams are filled with the shadow
Black block
Parents dreams are crippled by the sorrow
Black block
The beauty of our people never dies
Black block
You'll see it when you look into our eyes
Black block
Just take a moment breathe and look beyond
Black block
In front of you is what you thought was gone
Black block
Cos even when its gone it will remain
Black block
Things round here can never be the same

Bless

Local Resident, Artist, Poet, Activist (Green for Grenfell).

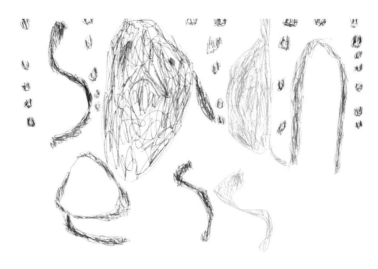

Lost Souls

Winsome Duncan a.k.a. Lyrical Healer

After 365 days the English skies are filled with Grenfell.

Lost souls, where are you now?

To meet such an ashy demise, the living
carry on in guilt ridden pain.

Corporate slaughter, mamine hundreds.
How can we safely sleep at night knowing what we know.

Injustice reigns and greed drives us to insanity.

Grenfell we still pray for you. As surrivors live on we wish you well.
Never forgotten.
Always forsaken.
We miss and love you all.

(C) Peaches Publications. 7th July 2018

Prominent Britiish spoken word artist and soulful singer.

Windows

Bex Tate

Hollow
eyes
once
windows
on
worlds
gaze blankly ..
burnt out
over
London
Town -
Profit
towers
high
above
anything
that
really matters.

54, Member of the public.

Beside The Fallen Ashes

Monera Takla

Wash it away with rain
Wash it away with heavy rain
Thundering on my window panes
Throw the flowers away the cards
That go on for yards
Hide it in blue builder's plastic
Ashes falling like fallen soldiers from the Second World War
On to my neighbour's gardens
The lost and fallen from the tower
Flowering into the gardens below
Blowing away with the wind
Walking past, not so fast
Old pictures of local families
No longer here to sit and drink their tea up there
Here we watch on listening to local MPS singing their song
Who's to blame they say ?
Yet help is delayed yet, another day
Blame, blame, blame every which way
Years of neglect government has to pay
Hide 'em in hotels
Maybe try move 'em to the end of the country if you let 'em
They won't let you forget them
This is not the end my friend
Our community will heal one day
But we ain't never walking away
Beside the fallen ashes.

39, Origin is English Mother and Egyptian father, born and raised in London.
Lost my younger brother 21 last year, which inspired my poetry.

Há Muita Coisa a Mudar

Braulio Barcelos

Vi onten na TV
Um tema sobre Grenfell
Que pena que dava
Que grande tristeza
A terra chorava
Tamanha tragédia
Vamos todos nos juntar
Porque há muita coisa a mudar

Yesterday I saw on TV
The news about Grenfell
It felt so sad
The World has gone mad
Mother Earth was crying
Because the whole building was burning
Let's all come together
To change the world for the better

This poem has been translated from Portuguese to English.

Grenfell Tower

Susan Juliana Samuel

There once used to be a diverse community
Of family and friends in the sky, in Grenfell Tower.
It has since after the fire, spread by its clad plastic wrappings
Become the Grave in the sky.
With its burnt charred Folks Spirits looming Free above,
Life no more.
Feelings of Sadness Remains.
To the Human Eye, You can feel their Despair, Fear, Pain and
Suffering .
These feelings cannot escape you.

RIP Dear Souls.

Local resident.

How Can I Tell You To Wipe Your Tears

Harriet Gore

How?
How?
How can I tell you?
How can I tell you to wipe your tears?
When I haven't wiped mine

It is not the failings that draw tears from my eyes,
For fallibility is a human condition and characteristics
It is not the failure to listen that keeps the tears flowing,
For obstinacy is a human condition and the characteristics of
diversity
It is not anger that I feel,
For my well of deep is flowing out reflections
The depth of deaths, no shallow can reveal

Everything was so perfectly aligned and allied, for the most
devastating catastrophe
The weather, the time, midnight and other factors
Like a natural disaster that was unnatural
Like a forest fire that was in a city
Like a shipwreck happening in a block

When it is death
Sometimes questions appear
Why like this?
Died too young
Oh, why now?

Who has the answers?
No one knows the answers
No answers know
Except that tears keep flowing

At first I cried for the dead
Their dreams and hopes and aspirations
Then I cried for the living, for the tears shed for the dead
In every tragedy, it is ourselves we cry for
Even when we cry for the dead and for the living
The dead do not need our tears
It is us who need healing
It is us who need our tears
The healing water which empties into the ocean of grief
To resurrect and to water, to moisten and to make fertile the heaving soil
To germinate seeds of hopes, dreams and aspirations which the dead have become
The manure which sprout spring when the first rain falls

The dead do not know they are dead, this is a consolation
Like that deep sleep when consciousness is lost
And all become nothing until consciousness returns
It is the living who know they are dead and cry for own selves
And feel for the dead what the dead does not feel
The dead are sleeping seeds, they are spreading scents,
They are evaporating into you and I and the space around
The dead have become the air we breathe, the words we disperse,
They have expanded into the expanse nothingness;
They have become the seeds which will germinate
when the first rain falls
Is this a consolation?
A consolation for the dead or for the living?

You see beloved one
Death is part of the story
The story on earth

The story earth tells
Tells about life
Life about death
Life is about death
Death is the destination of life
Once born, the destination is death
Death happens, just like life
Life is born just like death
Life is about living until death happens
Life is about occupying, engaging, serving,
Entertaining and feeding all our senses as best as we can until
death happens

Each death happens in its own way
Death is death
There is no uniform way of dying
Just as there is no uniform way of being born
Some are born by caesarean section and some are born legs firs
Some are born short and others born long
Some appear with hair and others appear bald
Some weigh 3kg and some 5kg at birth

When it is birth, joy appears on some faces
There is no one perfect time to be born
just as there is no one perfect time to die
No uniformity in birth and none in death
Each appears uniquely and disappears uniquely
Each enters this space in its own way
And exists as circumstances create

The present (here) is a story
The earth is a place of story telling
There is a life story and a death story
Some beginnings are exciting and some end in intrigue
Some leave quietly, some leave with a bang
Some lives are brief, some lives are long
What do we know, except, to question?

Who knows the answers?
Who knows why the flowers appear when they do and drop dead
when they do
Life is a story, telling itself, in its own way
Birth is part of the story and so is death
Some deaths are dramatic, some peaceful
And some are earthquakes appearing on the landscape
Volcanoes too and storms and sea wrecks
That is life, the life of a story, the life that is a story

I am listening to the sound when there is no sound
Except the sound of this
The thought that when entries are made into this space,
Many do not ask questions
about the appropriateness of the entries
But when exits are made, many questions become born
and appear to be asked

I write not to give hope for I have no hope to give
I write not to give comfort for I have no comfort to give
I only write to exhibit the me unseen
And reveal the conversation I have been having with myself
And the stream of tears which have become tributaries
The rivers of trails warming their way through
So how can I tell you to wipe your own tears,
when I have not yet wiped mine?
How can I tell you that all will be well,
when what was can never be is?
The many lives lost, a community in pain
Property can be replaced, but can new take the place of old?
Those who have gone, can they return?

How can I tell you to wipe your tears, when I have not wiped mine?
An invitation to write?
The question appears to be written?
What is the purpose of this writing?
Why write at all?

To give hope?
To console and to comfort?
To be on record as being a part of the many?
To tell people what they already know?
To make the difference only words make?
To express thoughts and add a voice?
To answer the call and support a beloved one?
To tell you to wipe your tears, when I have not yet wiped mine?
To tell you that those who have gone,
have become the formless writing the form you see?

In life, life is contained, in the form of forms
Outside that container, the form is formless spanning endless
Look at that form expanding into formless
What is it that is written in that distance?

"Some lives are long, some lives are brief?
The lives appeared, in form, the containers of life?
Outside the form, the formless expands?
Made in different forms, many become one book?
And the book of forms has become the formless unseen?"

You see beloved one
The formless has begun to write
In you and in me
Not just through words
But through thoughts and all expressions
In what is said
And what is unsaid
In the formless words
In the ink of the tears

So how can I tell you to wipe your tears, when the tears themselves
are the writings they wrote and the first raindrops to give life and
make fertile, bringing forth spring, the diverse rainbow
How can I tell you to wipe your tears,
when even at this moment I have not wiped mine?

Why wipe your tears when tears are still determined to flow?
Why stop your questions,
when questions are still determined to be heard?
Why did it happen?
How?
Remember beloved one, it is not anger that I feel,
For my well of deep is flowing out reflections

Everything was so perfectly aligned and allied,
for the most devastating catastrophe
The weather, the time, midnight and other factors
Like a natural disaster that was unnatural
Like a forest fire that was in a city
Like a shipwreck happening in a block
Leaving tears flowing in its wake
So how can I tell you to wipe your tears,
when I have not yet wiped mine?

I will wipe my face when there are no more tears flowing through
LOVE TO YOU ALWAYS
LOVE TO ALL ALWAYS

Version 7 August 2017

Founder Touch LOVE Worldwide
Written specially for inclusion in the 'Poetry4Grenfell compilation book'.
Special thanks to beloved Emmanuelle Marcel whose invitation inspired the
creation of this work.

Wonder If They Also Wake At Night

Karolina Hardy

Wonder if they also wake at night?
I can´t shut my wide eyed, freaked out eyes.
Like a child who just saw the most sinister of monsters.
No mother that can tuck me in and tell me it's gonna be alright.
I won't believe her.
Ever.
My trust shattered into pieces.
My heart hurts.
Wonder if they also wake at night?

Local resident, 46 year old mum of Eastern European heritage.

Swimming Pool Fire

Vienna Akins

Everybody knows about Grenfell Tower
Everybody in the world knows about Grenfell Tower
About the local fire brigade
And the burnt down
And the 300 men who are hot and dead
And the fire nearly touched the swimming pool
And the other towers near it
Jessica died and the man in the picture
With the big word that said MISSING
Mummy and daddy videoed themselves on the T.V
Out my bedroom window I saw smoke
The local fire brigade were making sure that people were safe
It nearly fell down
I feel sad because there's never been a fire before
That was the first fire in London
Grenfell Tower is really close to our house
And to our swimming pool
It looks like burnt bread

Age 5, North Kensington resident.

Never Forgotten

Keziah Davidge

Terror flowing through
Mountains of ash increasing
Trickling of blood
Pop of hope leaving
Bang of heart breaking
Heart-ache never healing
Fear taking over
Beat of sadness pulling you in
Lost never forgotten
Forever remembered

Year 8 student at Morpeth School, East London.

Name: Maya-louise
age: 10

Sadness

All of this grief i feel pain for the berieved i dislike all this
sadness, The residents and servivers not bein heard is
madness. The Survivers deserve to be heard Every day they
have to come back to the same place with nothing
that would put a smile on their face. The building
that they had ascaped from they cry den they here
the like a bridge song. For grenfell

tower ladbroke grove has the power
By Maya-louise
age 10.

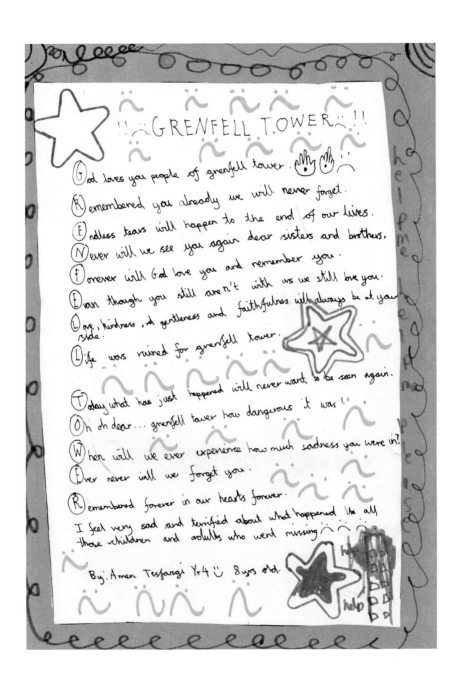

!!GRENFELL TOWER!!

G od loves you people of grenfell tower.

R emembered you already we will never forget.

E ndless tears will happen to the end of our lives.

N ever will we see you again dear sisters and brothers.

F orever will God love you and remember you.

E ven though you still aren't with us we still love you.

L ove, kindness, gentleness and faithfulness will always be at your side.

L ife was ruined for grenfell tower.

T oday what has just happened will never want to be seen again.

O h oh dear... grenfell tower how dangerous it was!

W hen will we ever experience how much sadness you were in?

E ver never will we forget you.

R emembered forever in our hearts forever.

I feel very sad and terrified about what happened to all those children and adults who went missing

By: Amen Tesfargi Yr4 ☺ 8 yrs old.

Good Samaritan

Ruth Reubens

When another suffers we look away
We will not pay will not stay
Specially if it is a stranger from another land
Why should we lend a hand?
Forgetting we are one family God is our father
We share the life of Jesus with Mary our Mother
A despised foreigner of another nation
Helped the robbed victim he knew his station
Priests and respected men had passed him by
They coldly ignored him to let him die
They pretended they had not seen his need
They followed their selfishness and greed
They ignore God's call into sin and they fall
If we are blinded by sin we cannot see
We would dwell in dark hell for eternity
For those who hate is their destiny

Prominent local resident, rasied by Catholic nuns.

My Best friend

Akeera Belfon-George

My best friend is a Grenfell Survivor.

Our journey started from Maxilla.

We rolled together from reception, and now in year 3,
Our friendship is stronger than ever.

What a mystery that night when your home was on fire
Caused by a faulty fridge wire.

I felt so sad thinking it was the end of our friendship,
But as a fighter, you survived the terrible trauma.

Hooray! You're here stronger than ever.

Year 3, St Thomas CofE Primary School (RBKC).

Super Me

Super me
I want to
be POW!
POW! ME!
I will kick
the baddies
in the face
I will jump
and win the
race. I will
make money into
honey to feed my and buy
bunny.

My
Super
Bunny
is Super
Funny.
We play
with kites
and have
a bite
of our
cookies
Super ME!

Morad

My Ninja friend.

In the night there is no light, You can see a moon with lots of room! I have a friend that's a ninja he only comes out at night so no one sees him, but he stays my bright. He has a pet snake that loves eating, cake! He's my friend friend because when its Ninja's are unusual

Morad.

Friendship

Friends: What are they? People who will care for you, people who will look out for you, people who will keep you safe, people who will always be there for you no matter what, they'll stick up for you.

What a true friend would do?
Make you laugh when you are sad, keep every promise, not keep secrets from you and help you along the way.

HOPE

FRIENDS

70

Forever together, never to part
Rarer than gold and more beautiful than art
In tough times, in hard times, you're always there
Everything you do shows that you care.
Nice as an angel is the love you show
Daring to care is the way that you go.

F.R.I.E.N.D.S
You're a true friend. You are the best.

My fabulous friend she's like a shooting star in the sky. I haven't seen her in ages. And I know she's a girl who never sheds a tear or shows a frown, but she's like a shooting star in the sky. She is safe but lives in a house but bragicly her cousin passed. I understand her sadness it would rather unkind of me to not comfort her.

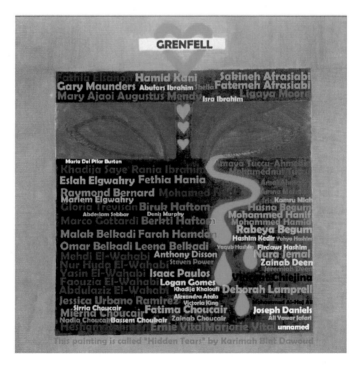

A Big Big Picnic

Carmen Akins

Grenfell Tower, Grenfell Tower
I love you, I miss you much
I don't like the way you burnt down
But I can get there
To make you all pretty
And make you good like you was
And paint you
So I can get you much cleaner as you was
I like the way you were painted before
I saw the fire on the newspaper when I was going to nursery
People got burnt down
And now they are in heaven
Some people got on the stairs
And then got on the pavement
Then they had no house
And they went to a big big picnic outside
And I went there too
We had pizza on the [Westway] floor
We had food and toys
With the girls that we saw
What were their names?
La La and Za Za?

Age 3 ½ , North Kensington resident.

My Family
_____

My family they are the best. When you ask for help
them, help you, I am happy God made
Hemen

141

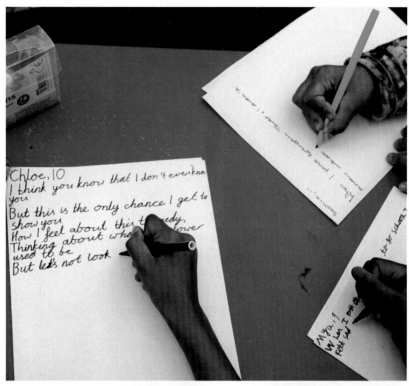

The Dragon's Fire

Elijah Jacob Aldea
Co-Author Gabrielle Sonia Ali

(excerpt of book)

Page 1
A huge flame came out from a cave on Rocky Mountain in Apo Forest. It was a mix of dazzling oranges, yellows and reds and lit up the night sky.
The flame belonged to Freddy the dragon. He lived all alone and every night a bright light shone out from the cave.

Page 2
Freddy was very lonely and longed to have some friends.
But every time he tried to say hello a big ferocious flame would come out of his mouth and scare everyone away.
He didn't know what to do!!
He really wanted to be friends with Pedro the monkey. Everyone liked Pedro, he was always laughing and happy. He had lots of friends but Pedro was afraid of Freddy's big flame, and ran away whenever Freddy came near.

Page 3
This made Freddy very sad, as he did not know why he couldn't make friends.
He tried to be friendly and say hello but all the animals in Apo Forest always ran away whenever he came near.
He felt so sad and lonely that he couldn't stop the tears from falling and went back into his cave on Rocky Mountain, where he decided we would stay from now on....

Page 9
....Freddy now had clay slabs all around his cave where he could

easily communicate with his friends. He no longer got frustrated that no one could understand him.

He was as happy that everyone accepted him and was no longer afraid of him. That night as all of his friends slept, Freddy no longer cried tears of sadness but Intears of joy.

In memory of
ELIJAH JACOB ALDEA
10/02/2004: 19/11/2017

The Dragon's Fire is a story about being "different" for children. This book provides comfort, reassurance and strength to children who may be bullied, ostracised or has a disability of any form and find it hard to "fit-in". It teaches them that they are special, unique and loved. It gives hope that even though things might be hard at first, there is always a way if they don't give up.

The first half of this book was written by my son Elijah Jacob Aldea, who sadly passed away on 19/11/2017, after being left severely disabled after a medical incident. Much love, care and thought has been poured into this book. I hope this book will help children cope with life's difficulties and being "differently- abled". Elijah cared passionately about people and children, especially those who couldn't fend for themselves. He wanted to take away their pain a lot of the time, if not all of the time. He always encouraged and prayed, for people to be brave, strong and courageous.

"...Be strong and courageous. Do not be afraid; do not be discouraged, for the LORD your God will be with you wherever you go"
Joshua 1:9
"BE BRAVE"

www.elijahsmiracles.com

The Voices of Grenfell Tower

Alemu Tebeje

ሃሹምም ይጣራል! ይጣራል! ይጣራል!
የባለቤቴም ድምጽ፣ ይጣራል! ይጣራል!
የሶስት ልጆቼም ድምጽ፣ ይጣራል! ይጣራል!
ህንፃ ኔሪ አቃጥሎ፣ ያ ጨካኝ ነበልባል፣
አሁንም ባሳቤ፣ ሁልዬ ይነዳል፣
አዎ አሰማለሁኝ፣ የሚነዱ ድምፆች፣ ከተቃጠሉት፣
ከአጻገ ወጣቶች፣ ባልቴት፣ አዛውንት፣
አዎ! ማርኮም አለ! ይጣራል! ይጣራል!
የወንዱች፣ የሴቶች፣ የማወቃቸው ሁሉ ድምፃቸው ይሰማል፣
አዎ! የዘይነባም!   ይጣራል! ይጣራል!
ካውቶቡስ ማቆሚያው፣ ሰላም ጎረቤቴ፣ እንደት አደርክ ይላል፣
በርናርድም ይጣራል! ይጣራል! ይጣራል!
ላቲመር መንገድ ላይ፣ አባቡሩ ጣቢያ፣ ብዙ ተያይተናል፣
የቱራም ይጣራል! ይጣራል! ይጣራል! ይጣራል!
የሰቆቃ ድምፆች ከሚነዱ ስልኮች ጎልቶ ያስተጋባል፣
የሃኒያ፣ የኢዛዲራም፣ ይጣራል! ይጣራል!
ስለደረጃዎች፣ ስለጥቅጥቅ ጭሱ፣ ማሬን ይናገራል፣
ዓይናቸው ቢፈስም፣ ስለህንፃው ቋያ አሁን ለመመስከር፣
በአካልም ቢለዩ፣ በውስጡ ከመኖር፣
እንቶነም ይጣራል! ይጣራል! ይጣራል!
መልካም ሰላምታቸው፣ ከፊገግታቸው ጋ መንገድ ላይ ይመጣል፣
አዎ! የማሪያም ይጣራል! ይጣራል! ይጣራል!
ከጭሱ ጋር አብሮ፣ የሁሉም ነፍሳቸው ወደላይ አርጓል
        ጮርቃው ጀረማያም! ይጣራል! ይጣራል!
መንደርተኛ ሆነን፣ ለመታት ኖርናል፣
ይኸው አሁን ደገሞ፣ ስለ አሟሟታቸው ዋቢ አድርገውኛል፣
ከሚነዱ ነፍሶች፣ የሚነዱ ድምፆች፣ ሁሌ ይሰሙኛል፣
ብዕርህ ስለሃቅ፣ ይመስክር ይሉኛል፣
የሊጋያ ድምፁዋ፣   ይጣራል! ይጣራል!

መጺሃም ይጣራል! ይጣራል! ይጣራል!
ስለ ፖርብትናህ ምን አደረከ ይላል፤
ሁልዬም ስወጣ ድምፆቸ ይጮኻሉ፤
ዘወትር ስገባም ለማወቅ ይሻሉ፤
በክብሪት ሳጥን ውስጥ፤ ለምንድን ታፖረው እንደተቀጠሉ፤
የተነዉ መኖሪያ ቤት፤ ፍትህ ያለ ብለዉ ሁሌ ይጠይቃሉ፤
የኑራም ቤተሰብ፤   ድምፃቸዉ ይጮኻል፤
ከድጃና እናቲ፤ ድምፃቸዉ ይሰማል፤
የማላከም ድምፁ፤ የጀሲካ ድምፁዋ፤ ትኩም አብሮ ድምፁ
የበሩክ፤ የናቱ፤ የዓሊ፤ የይሳቅ ድምፅ፤ የዚያ የቀንበጡ
ይጣራል! ይጣራል!
ይጣራል! ይጣራል! ይጣራል!   ይጣራል! ይጣራል!

(የእንግሊዝኛ ትርጉም በክሪስ ቤኬት)

Hashim is calling calling
Hashim's wife is calling calling
Hashim's three children are calling calling
Look! The fire consumed a building
Now it is consuming me
With all the burning voices of the dead
Old people young people
Marco is calling calling
Boys and girls everyone I used to see
Zainab is calling calling
And say hello to at the bus stop
Bernard is calling calling
Or the train station on Latimer Road
Nura is calling calling
Voices wailing into their twisted mobiles
Hania and Esra are calling calling
About the stairs and the smoke
Even if they have no eyes to see the building
Or live in it now without their bodies
Anthony is calling calling
Even if their kind words and smiles in the street
Mariem is calling calling

Have all gone up in smoke
Jeremiah is calling calling
We shared this ground
Now I bear witness to their disappearance
Oh! Burning souls have burning voices
Let me be their guarantee of truth!
Ligaya is calling
Medhi calling
We lived next door... What will you do for us?
The voices ask whenever I go out
Or come back home they want to know
Why it burnt down in minutes like a matchbox
And where will I find justice and a home
For Nura's family of voices
Khadija's family of voices
For Malak's voice and Jessica's and Tuccu's
For Biruk and his mother's voice and Ali's voice and little Isaac...
Calling calling calling calling calling calling calling

Originally Translated from Amharic into English by Chris Becektt.

The Promise

Debbie Golt

I have a new companion
That sits lightly on my shoulder
Not always in attendance
But always in mind
Grief and I have come to a new understanding
I have come to accept
Its presence
Its presence
I will never forget
I don't want to
I always remember
I choose to
Cherish all of you
Especially one
Especially
I won't dwell on regret
I don't need to
I know that I will have moments
When I will be overcome
With the feelings
And thus I will
No longer be taken by surprise
In return Grief has promised me
Not to ambush
Not to knock me sideways
Just when I am on my feet
Or when I see a family
Complete, and enjoying
Otherwise innocuous pleasures
Strolling together
Not to trigger
Uncontrollable sadness

At the slightest thing
Or at the crossroads
And to welcome my mission
Which must be sacred
As I am still here
And I push

Sometimes I think I am
The more honourable partner
I have kept
My side
Of
The bargain

April 2017

Mother, DJ, poet.

Tell Them

Monera Takla

Tell them
Tell his mum he is not returning
Tell his school his students will no longer be learning
Tell his colleagues his team are no longer
Tell his wife their sons are no more.
Tell her child daddy is still up there
Tell his school he has gone.
Tell his grandfather his home is gone.
Tell her best friend she is no more.

39, Local resident, origin is English Mother and Egyptian father, born and raised in London. Lost my younger brother, 21 last year, which inspired my poetry.

Migration

Emily Souza Macanita

We once lived a happy life,
But then we got attacked by people with knives.
We got taken away,
I haven't seen my family since today.
Tears of joy transported to another place,
This happy memory I shall never erase.
Yet I still suffer in this camp,
Just think of good things and your life won't be damp.

10 year old of a Portuguese/Angolan and Brazilian background.

Grenfell ~ A Circle of Shrines

AamaSade Shepnekhi

There's A Circle Of Shrines Around Grenfell
A Moat Of Water And Light
Catching Spirits Directing Their Energies
I See Angel Wings At The Shrines
Come To Collect The Souls
Who At First Didn't Realise They Needed To Go

I Feel The Breeze Of The Wings
As They Embrace
All Who Need Comfort In This Grenfell Disaster

I Sense The Impossible Task Ah Clearing Away
So Life Can Live On Day To Day
I Hear The Everlasting Stories
Of Human Man-Kind Spirit Divine
As They Rise In Glory Political Reputations Plummet

I Circle The Shrines
Packing Donation Boxes From Baby Clothes To Bread
Grieving Strangers And Survivors
Mourning The Missing Dead

Congregating In Comeunity
Healing Artistic Spaces Created
So Much Heartical Charity
Turning Away Donations & Media Attention
Sick And Tired Of Their Storytelling
There Is Angels Wings At The Shrines
Keeping The Light Bright

So Wondering Souls
Find A Way To Peace

I Circle The Shrines
Calling Ancestors Come
Liberate Your Relations Please
So Outa Calamity Come Harmony

Ancestral Spirits Of The Families
Come - Claim Youre Children
So All Who Suffer Find A Likkle Ease
And Those Snatched Away Find Peace

I Ask The Most High To Forgive Transgressions
Of Those Who Crossed The Veil Of No Return
Let Their Karma Be Balance
So They Can Assist Us
Their Spirit Lives On
To Make Sense Of This Tragedy
And Heal Ourselves, Our Families

It so Sad It Took A Tragedy
To Wake Us From Our Slumber
People From All Walks Of Life And Culture
Let's Hold Onto This Expression Of Immense People Power
Let's Remember Impossible Means I'm Possible
Let's Look Into Our Neighbour's Eyes
An Smile A New Dawn Is On The Rise
We Can Never Give Up On Grenfell
Or Any Other Disaster

All The Names Of Those Lost
Will Not Be In Vain
Cannot Forget You
The World Will Never Be The Same
Without You

Angel's Wings Reside At The Shrines
Comforting The Souls
So Many Have Flown
Feel The Breeze Of The Wings As They Embrace
Comforting - Holding - Reassuring
We In Unity Pour Water On This Corporate Fire
So Shed Your Tears Lets Pour Water On The Ground
Libation - Let Our Word-Sound Release
That Justice Compassion And Truth Abound

I Invite You Continue To Circle The Shrines
With Your Spirit Heart And Mind
Pay Homage To Those Brave Victims
Of A System Who See Numbers Not Humans
Let's Continue To Pour Water
Quench This Disaster

There's A Circle Of Shrines Around Grenfell
Tell Me! What Is Your Plan?
Western Civilised Kinda-Man!
Yu See I Continue To Circle Shrines
Singing Songs Of Redemption
And Singing The Songs Of Emancipation
Ashè

- Local resident, Shamanic Celebrant, Storyteller and Percussionist, August 2017.

In Plain Sight

Joy

At night...
When I listen to the Rhythm of the Free,
The human's emotion of you and me;
It is Injustice I think of from night to day:
Conquest not justice is the evil that pervades,
A better off society 2 Miles from Grenfell Estate.

It is justice not conquest all like-minded (people) seek,
For the wicked do not sleep.
Their wickedness keeps a plain sighted vision:
Our Love for the fallen and for the Living
Breathes in daylight,
As humbling reason, vistas shows,
The Grenfell we once knew:
A vibrant constellation of people;
Never to be forgotten.

And we always celebrate each life as if it were our own,
For we are bound in our memories, our days and our nights:
And will always remember in silence and in noise;
The people of Grenfell their cats, their dogs, their toys.
As a community of fellow travellers in and out of life,
Gone but never Forgotten ...

"This is my tribute. My family and I lost two very close friends, every time we think about it you'll find us crying. It is beyond admirable what you and your colleagues have organised. You have my full support".

Boxes and Goodies

Mary Gardiner

Boxes and boxes
Lorries and vans
Are now what is needed
For this poor damaged land

It is now filled with goods so plentiful
We could clothe and feed two worlds full of people

It's not needed now
Or ever more
Money will be paid
To ease the sore
And wounded
The Lost and grieving
And should we
Could we
Ask for more?

Please sir???

I wrote these pieces after the fire.

The Groove of the Grove

Tammy Samede

I cannot recall the first moment, I fell in love with this place,
Perhaps it was one summer evening at Maxilla chatting,
Learning about its different people and cultures,
But I know I have been feeling the groove of the grove,
Carving its own grooves into my heart, imprinted forever,
Like a handprint on the sands of time, immoveable and deep,
Flows my feelings for its community,
its unique flow and frequency.

Maybe I fell in love with this place, whilst watching its local artists,
Paint into life murals and faces, in the community spaces,
Each brush stroke, stroking my soul, painting itself,
Talking about the history and histories, colourful and vibrant,
Streaked with struggle amid the colourful lives.

Maybe I fell in love with this place, when I
recognised more faces than not,
Maybe it was in every hello, high-five and cuddle,
smile of recognition,
But somewhere between the first nod of a formal greeting,
And the more recently typical cuddles, I fell..... totally in love.
It could have been on Portobello road, getting to know the stalls,
Finding my way through the streets here, carving my path,
The shouts of people laughing and teasing, and
My own growing resentment at the toffs "stealing our stuff!!!"
Maybe it was somewhere between
the first days of pain and chaos,
And the volunteering for those who became family and friends,
At some point I stopped saying "this community",
And started to feel protective, loving and warmer for the people.

I don't know when I first fell in love,
With the people and the places,
The sounds and the wonderful faces,
The art and community spaces,

But I fell,
And when I fell I surrendered,
And I learned that the colour of love,
Is green...

Local resident.

One Week After

Mary Gardiner

The Hurley burley is over
The praying is done
The sun is out
But where have we gone?

What did we learn?
What did we do?
Have lots of folk died
For me and for you?

Is there a God?
I do not know
And don't either care
All I know
Is lots of babies are not here
Relatives of loved ones shedding tears

Death defies us
Over and over
And when all is said
Nothing is done.

Let us hope and hope and push on more
And never go back to those days of yore.

I wrote these pieces after the fire.

Chloe, 10

I think you know that I don't even know you
But this is the only chance I get to show you
How I feel about this tragedy,
Thinking about what that tower used to be
But let's not look at the past now
We'll just figure out how
To come back even stronger
Because now your life is longer
And the amber alert, I know you are hurt
But we can find them with the work
The panic and doubt won't last foreva
Because we're strong as one, stronger together

Frost's Thoughts

David 'Frost' Ellison

If money is power, I say tax is fuel!

They say time is a healer, and that love conquers all. I ask how?
How can time heal our hearts after seeing loved ones fall!
I've loved my area for over 25 years
and will continue to love her always,
So why does my love or yours not conquer the pain that has been
left in west 10?
I say because we have been lied to,
Forced to believe that they hold all the power.
I say they don't!
United we are Strong,
together we will and shall overcome anything
No matter what life throws at us!

My heart , love and condolences go out to my ends and each and
every one of you that has lost family or friends.

Local resident and old skool rapper from Grove.

Grenfell Trauma

Shareefa Energy

Still processing all witnessed since early hours this morning
Local block of flats enflamed and burning
The screams of grown men and children
Men waving clothes from windows
Rubble and debris spinning through the sky
and falling like dead crows
Still processing what this all means to the local community
What it means for the child I cuddled to my side
Whilst he breathed through his oxygen mask
For the fathers sitting in soaked clothes from the hose
In shock not wanting to register having lost their children
Men in tears for losing their wives
People frantic as to whether they would see again their child
A woman struggling to breathe and growing hysterical
When hearing news of her husband she couldn't find
Men with cuts on their feet from the force of falling
With hundreds of people pushing for their life
Holding the emotion down, be strong don't get emotional now
The trauma of seeing a blazing building hours later
Looking like a giant rotting corpse
Memories of police trying to move us
Friends coming to meet us with blankets
To remove clothes of the drenched and quivering
Praying and hoping the elder who wants me to meet his wife,
Praying we hear news she is still alive
An hour's sleep after being on the street from 3 to 10am
Waking up drenched in sweat, shaking in uncontrollable sobs
Wondering how deeply my local community
who witnessed all unfold
Or currently on the streets will feel this
Typing with shaking hands

How long will this trauma linger
What will the funerals look like
How is this community to recover from the truth of hearing people
screaming When being burnt alive
Processing, faces flashing before me
Bodies being brought out on stretchers
Assisting paramedics
Handing out water and blankets
All in disbelief and knowing the reasons behind the fire expanding
Knowing the gentrifies and ill-wishers
intending to ethnically cleanse the flats
Easy targets, no sign of a powerful hose to put out the fire
A bigger spray of water only to be seen hours later
Praying those affected are able to recover
Sending love and healing to all in close relation to Grenfell Tower

Local resident and poet, originally from Leicester.

A Nocturne for Grenfell

David Wingfield

You will be remembered,
Voiceless victims, whose wild cries shattered our slumber,
As leonine flames charred the cloudless sky,
Your roar was deafening.

You will be remembered,
Your fear-white faces illuminated
the beacon that blotted out the light,
Waving, now goodbye,
your window-paned prison refused release,
You stayed put, far beyond every heroism,
Watching, with time-frozen stoicism, and without wing,
Un-consoled in the uncontrolled lashing of tongues,
Until sequestered by its febrile plumes:
Your sitting rooms, now profane tombs,
Within a gaudy pyre.

You will be remembered,
Fragile martyrs of midsummer,
Mass-immolated on Mammon's filthy altar,
Whose blackened skeleton,
Now ugly, now ashamed,
Groans for justice, bereft of peace.

You will be remembered,
Lives on your spirit, furiously flame-retardant,
Without need of ersatz cladding,
Your promises, no bitter products of combustion savaged,
Will find a new life,
Will breathe a crisp air, once denied.

You will be remembered:
When we build new towers,
With concrete of community,
And steel of self-forgetting,
Where cost will not be counted, and penthouses will be priceless:
At last, a loved home fire-proof,
where you and your friends may dwell.

And under June's balmy nights,
You will be remembered,
You will be remembered.

Vice Principle at Bassett House School, W10.

This Black Post

Rich Pierce

Put me in a high rise putting paid to my life
Caged the rage when you cannot be saved
For air's all I care just to be down there
Solid ground the sound of never more profound
My 9 11 on 6 14 Uncanny No's as they add up
You see 20 20 vision upon your television
Rescue is futile hear the howls of derision

Phone calls to mum Live streams on media as our lives ebbed away
We waved at the windows Sit down Children it's all going to be ok
As smoke billowed down the hallway Can anyone of you imagine
Ending your days screaming I've not lived!
And My dreams what of they?

Just to walk amongst nature in spring with a spring in my step
God's praises I'd sing Family close to have and to hold
I'd want for nothing never complain of the cold
Why oh why with our lives did they play
My oh my someone's gonna pay ...
To The Shoreditch crew Battersea too called too late what could
you do
But the first on the scene what's this we have seen on the BBC
Inadequecy
On Panorama unfolds more drama the fire was put out
I beg your pardon
We shout As the program ended top ladders extended
By now all is lost but how small the cost

To go and get the proper kit met their match when it re-lit ...
The 'have-nots' the 'haves' let's believe can heal
the rifts and the other perceive

For all your wants and for all your needs
For happiness and peace and the air that that you breathe.

This Black Post,
The Ghosts
With eyes so blue

Look down on you

Fire Kit

Selina Zekarias

Grenfell tower was a beautiful place,
But there was only one thing that they couldn't ace,
That terrible thing was the fire kit,
And that's how the Grenfell fire hit.

Shouts of help and screams of terror!!
The burning fire was a complete error,
Leaving the sky all black and damp,
Trying to get attention by switching their lamp.

Seeing their faces made me upset,
All of this is like a big threat,
Everyone will try to help to the best,
All of them were really stressed.

May God look after them and help any of them
that haven't already recovered.
Oh mighty Lord please help them
and cure them for anything that hasn't gone well.

Aged 9.

My Tower

Naomi Sylvester

This was my tower,
Now it's no more
Flames rose up like a ferocious beast
Causing panic and making all confused,

How I wish it was an illusion,
As we tried to escape from this disaster
My heart now filled with misery and depression
Thinking in my heart if I will survive tomorrow

My dear Lord I cry,
Who would like to smile once again
Please don't let me die
As I walked through the unbearable and disastrous smoke,
All I could do is fumble, as I started to choke
After shouting several times to save my families
A fireman comes to do what he supposed to do best
Even though they should have done more to save more lives

Now some of them have escaped, we feel really glad
But still feel extremely heartbroken
My heart cries out with sorrow
For those who will not see tomorrow

Oh Grenfell Tower, Oh Grenfell Tower, how majestic you once were
After the twenty third hour of burning,
you now look like a dead flower
All those memories of loved ones are now just ashes
Just left memories in our heads, not seeing their graves.

Aged 10.

No Time To Admire

Rachel Sylvester

Sleeping peacefully in my bed
Pillow hopefully supporting my head
Suddenly, I heard my neighbour shouting fire, fire....
Grenfell Tower no time to admire

In the midnight smoke everywhere
People wanting for open air
This intense heat and filing smoke in my lungs
We saw fire tones and tones

People risking their lives on the staircase
Trying to get a bit of airspace
Flames more and more
Fire smoke as I opened the door

Money saving risking life
Making cladding never strives
Unstoppable, unbearable and undesirable moment
We don't have any time to comment

But what can I expect
Grenfell Tower wrecked

Oh!!! What a helpless moment for me
Fire as my opponent

I can feel the pain; I can hear the scream from babies,
children and adults
In an hour of sorrow what is the result?

Heart breaking and pain
And smoke blocking my veins in this Grenfell Tower

Burning, burning Grenfell Tower
Fire putting more and more power
Grenfell tower was my home
Now we're just going into a room

Aged 9.

Together We Rise

Rishma Dhaliwal

My eyes drip with water as I shut them tight and feel their pain.
My heart feels heavy as the sound of cries for help ring in my ear...
The loss of lives, memories flickering away, turning to dust.
All that remains is the gripping of the hands of strangers,
Holding on tight,
As they find comfort in the arms of those who
understand their suffering.
Because their voices failed to be heard,
Their screams will forever mark their territory.
Their tower will continue to be the home of their
smiles, laughter and love.

Together they rise to rebuild their land,
As we watch the dripping blood from the
government's "helping" hand.

Poet and founder of I Am Hip-Hop magazine.

Forever in our Hearts

Sofia Dadou

This was their home not long ago
And now it drops in plight
A symbol of tragedy -
But, their strength stands in height
Family, friends and community
Brought further together:
They stand as an army to help -
A symbol of strength forever

A new home is made in our hearts
Filled by love of those who were lost
We are reminded to cherish every hour
Those beautiful people will transcend
That ugly building -
And whilst that will be taken down,
These souls will ascend

As the golden sun rises,
It illuminates the tower
- an animated thought that
They forgot to turn the lights off.
The sun smiles as it ruminates
Those zestful hours of living,
And again, it smiles at seeing us open new gates:
And that we must remember for them.

12 year old that lost a friend in the fire. This poem is dedicated to those lost in the fire: victims, survivors, their extended families and the Grenfell Community.

The Sea

Emily Souza Macanita

The Fresh air flies by
You get great gasp from the sky

The sea dances slowly in the distance
The sun sets at an instant

The breath-taking view sends you in shocks
While you are sitting by the docks

The soft golden sand sways in the wind
Then suddenly appears a happy grin!

10 year old of a Portuguese/Angolan and Brazilian background.

I Got Faith In You

Lion'el – Marcel- Raphael Jabbour

Please God don't let the people remember how they died in the fire.
I got Faith in U.
You created Life and You Created Death,
I thank you every day from my first to last breath

*Ankh-Wdja-Snb
**Ashe'...

6 year old local resident, son of life-long RBKC resident and poet
- Y1, Kensington Primary Academy

* Translated from Metu Neter (Ancient Egyptian Language):
Life-Prosperity-Health
**"What will be will be / Let it be so" in the Yoruba language

Bare Feet

Oisín

You would ask for the moon.
To light your path.
You would look for a bright way through the streets of London.
Where the fish man has fresh fish.
And the black ducks take flight from the lily pads on the River Lea.
And in this early morning.
I would wish all of this for you.

11 Year old.
Dedicated to the children of the Grenfell Tower Tragedy 2017
This poem won a prize in last year's Foyle Young Poets!

Ability

Kinetic Kizitta
(Kizitta Anning)

Ability is Opportunity
Grab it in its Entirety
Express it in Simplicity
Ability gives Chances
For Destiny
Ability isn't Vanity
When Explored for Growth
Ability Defines your Identity
Let the Opportunity
Bring you Unveiling Possibilities
Adorned with Grace
You will understand
That Ability is an Immense Opportunity

Poet, Singer, Inspirational Speaker, Performance Artist, Fashion Statement.

The Voices Will Speak Again

By Nahiyan Alam

Wash away the pain
Who is there to blame?
Will there be a next day?
Someone will pay
The community will not walk away
The thundering cries have no delay
How many days will be grey?
How many of us were oblivious?
The sour taste of ashes were emotionally destructive
Soon happiness will rise again
Soon the people will heal
Soon the voices will need to speak again

*Inspired by Monera Takla's 'Beside The Fallen Ashes', Year 8
student at Morpeth School, East London.*

Spirits Live in the Air

Monera Takla

The air is silent around Grenf...
The blackbirds sing from the treetops on high
The air is stifly silent
We hear the childrens' cries, cries.
Turn on the radio and T.V. to hear the lies, lies.

The people we loved and knew are in the air everywhere
We are keen to show we care, we care
We love them
We want justice for our friends, mums, neighbours, dads, uncles,
aunts, brothers, nans, Grandads, babies yet to come
These feelings can never be undone.

Their spirits live in the air
Everywhere
How we want to know the truth
Although it may never undo the damage that has been done
The truth is where will we go from here?
Yet full of fear
Too weary from shedding tears

We do care
We do care
Don't just stop and stare taking pictures here and there without a
care !
This isn't the place
Give the people their space, space.
Children we love, friends we love, are resting there
Don't just walk without a care or just stop and stare
Think of the innocent souls we love who are way on high up above
in the tower.

Young lives still not yet in bloom
Left us all too soon, too soon
Their only crime, no silver spoon

Old and young gone before their time, time
For them the clock no longer chimes
Never, ever, ever let this happen again, again

The eyes, the eyes
The cries, the cries from the Grenfell tower
The unborn babies yet to flower
Only we have the power for change
To make the government re-arrange
Don't just turn the page

Don't try to gather in rage
Time for change
It is too late for them
This can never happen again.

The eyes, the eyes
The cries,the cries
The blame, the blame
The shame, the shame
This can never happen again

21.6.17

39, Local resident, origin is English Mother and Egyptian father, born and raised in London. Lost my younger brother, 21 last year, which inspired my poetry.

In the dark of night

In the dark of night, there will be light.
Everything is bright even at the dark of night.
At day it is always bright, but in the dark of night...

The dark spreads itself reaching everyone but even at the dark of night
The light still appears.
In the dark of night there will be light... forever.

Dark with night, light with day
Dark and night never beat light.

Bye Elias Chaffin

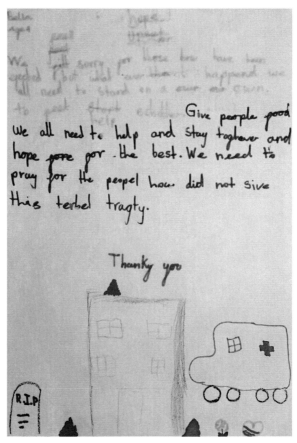

We all need to help and stay together and
hope for the best. We need to
pray for the peopel how did not sive
this terbel tragty.

Give people good

Thank you

R.I.P

Sophia, 11

When I past Grenfell Tower, I didn't
know what to exept from all that
say
happiness from the tower must
had faded away. All I can do
is pray each and everyday. For all
those people living on the edge
in
only dreaming of a bed. Family lost
for ever now, all we want to know
is how. When I see the ash's fall
all I ask for is joy as sadness
should never know know you
always around
alone as it will be in your life
down
all the time. So keep your head
held high as happiness will
come around.

HOPE

Eden
9

Grenfell is sad it's
really bad. A fire in our
community. Grenfell is a
tragedy. May the ones lost in the
Perlouis flames rest in peace forever
and, always. We must pray the
Lord we'll shed some to to the
people. people

Some say before you are born your life is written in the books of destiny, yet whilst there is breath in your body the words are ones you are not privileged to see. When you sense you know your future and feel lost and misery, know you do not have access to that legendary library. Dig deep and take a breath with me and know this time will pass. You are stronger than you thought you could ever be, never settle with injustice, live and love as if each breath is your last. The journey can be a long one, built for those that are steadfast. If your path is broken then today cast a new path. When the time comes to read your life be content with time past.

Marc Compton

Butterflies
    Can't catch them for long.
        Or they will die.
But
    if they fly free
    they colour in the sky
        and the leaves.

Flutter flutter clours in our hearts
~~Don't chase too~~ we chase they flee
~~too~~ We sit, they tiptoe up~~to~~ our
arms
Flutter flutter colours in our breath
Stutter stuttered ~~they~~ heartbeats guide
    our words
~~flattered flattered colors~~
utter word utter you utter I
Fly like the colours, ~~your~~ our words belong
    to the sky

HOPE

How One People Elevate
~~How Our Perspective Expands~~
How ~~Own~~ OUR Perseptions Evolve
Hope is Heading Over persection
it's not just a noun, ~~effortless~~
it's a verb, to Hope
and when we put our hope
in action we can turn
poision into medicine
We can rise above any border
We can overcome every opression
Hope is Holding Onto Positive Emoti
it is Having Oneness Pulsating Everywhere
It is How Our perspective expands
from Impossible to I'm Possible.

Hope is

HELPING ONESELF + PROPELLING
EVERYONE

It is

HAVING OPENESS, PROPOGATING EQUALITY
It is the begining of
HOW ~~ONES~~ OUR PROBLEMS END.

We Are Survivors

Tasfia Khan

The fire burns, smoke in the air,
The people weep, full of despair.
Falling fast in the heavy drops of rain,
No amount of water can wash out the pain.

Some were lost, some were found,
Only a few of us are safe and sound.
Angry, neglected, they were left alone,
No one knows the pain of losing a home.

The crack in our hears we'll have to seal,
But don't worry, with time we will heal.
We are the survivors, so strong my friend,
Together, I believe we can make it to the end!

*Inspired by Monera Takla's 'Beside The Fallen Ashes', Year 8
student at Morpeth School, East London.*

Mehtageen Taghyeer
We Need Change

EmpresS *1 aka (الامبراطورة الاولي)

Mehtageen taghyeer fel wad3 el ehna fee
Mehtageen taghyeer fel wad3 el ehna fee

محتاجين تغير في الوضع اللي احنا فيه

Daroori we mengher takheer lel wad3 el ehna feee,
Mehtageen taghyeer fel wad3 el ehna fee

ضروري ومن غير تأخير للوضع اللي أحنا فيه
محتاجين تغير في الوضع اللي احنا فيه

We need change, to the situation that we're in
We need change, to the situation that we're in
Urgently and without delay
To the situation that we're in
We need change, to the situation that we're in!

Excerpt of song - originally written, recorded and filmed during and after the Egyptian Revolution 2011-2012 Producer and Arranger: Ital 12 Productions With musicians: Sarah Tobias, Leroy 'Mafia' Heywood, Folo Graff, Winston Reedy.

On Youtube: @Empress1Egypt We Need Change

Angels in the Sky

Bianca Gordon

At 32 minutes past the midnight hour,
Heavens gates opened at the Grenfell tower.
Innocent lives lost, sister, mother, brother,
We saw humanity care for one another.
The community strength was immediately present,
People from all over came to help in an instant.
Such tragic news, we must come together,
Spread our love, light and prayers,
Remember forever.

At 32 minutes past the midnight hour,
heavens gates opened at the Grenfell tower.
At 32 minutes past the midnight hour,
heavens gates opened at the Grenfell tower.

27, from Enfield, of Jamaican and English heritage.

"I wrote this the day after it happened, the whole tragedy has had me in floods of tears when I think of all the innocent people that lost their lives that night.

There have been many horrible things going on in the UK, I really felt like this took the "great" out of Britain.

I found it hard to emotionally connect with some events that took place prior to this, the Grenfell tower tragedy tore my heart right out of me, I felt the sadness and hurt from where I was, I believe that all of humanity are connected in some out of this world type of way, I really feel this .

I wish there was more I could do to help.
I wish the survivors all the best from the bottom.

MY Jesus!

Miad

I'm as lucky as can be for the worlds
best Lord belongs to ME!

He's the one who makes the sun shine. † He's the
one who makes the moonlight! †
He's the one who makes the stars shine Bright †
And he's the one who Jesus you make everything
bright!
my star! My best friend!

JESUS

Acknowledgements

Th'ankh you to:

The Most High Creator, all the Saints and my Ancestors.

My mama Malika Amal and all my family that have supported me.
Romeo, Pascal, Bernard, Baba, Lion'el-Marcel, Braulio and Igor.
The beloved Harriet Gore from Touch Love Worldwide
Rebekah Raphael - One Love Grove
Neleswa - Community Relief
Shirine - Colourtrail
Mahlet R, Ayo, Joy
Siobhan and Joe - Maxilla
Steve, Keni, Jason and Brendon - EPIC
Lucy, Suzy, Josh and Osei - Henry Dickins
Gary Thomas, Zetta, Ruth, Jason & Phil - Westway Trust
Tom Fitch - CASH
Maxwell - T Shirts and tech help
Suzel Pitty and Miranda – K & C Arts Dept.
Matthew Keane – CLLL and Abingdon Ward Councillors
JB – Portobello Film Festival
Gino and Zita
Octavia Foundation - Andrew, Conor, Martha
KPA and WLFS
LBHF and the Councillors
Lorraine Williamson - Nu Dawn
Monique - Opera Holland Park
Amanda Beckles and Laurelle - GTCMP
Toby Laurent and Belson - Green 4 Grenfell
Yvette and Moyra - Justice for Grenfell
Amon Saba - Karnak House
Shaun Clarke, Leroy Al-Aswani, Mike Medas, Iesha Slater,
Vanessa Downie and Antony Marcano
Ishmahil Blagrove
MTink and Portobello Novella - Matt and Jaqi
All the Volunteers - Yago, Mahlet, Rhonda, Giulia, Jose, Isis, Andreia
My camera man Igor

Ash Kotak and Alla Dryzhak for first film edit
Eli Zheleva - for all her time creating the Kamitan Arts website
Ahmed 'Don X' el Dady - Poetry 4 Grenfell logo
Mark Antony - Revival Pictures W10 CIC for further film edits
Matthew Phillip - The Tabernacle space for our debut book exhibition
Maya Matanah - LoveVegan cuisine
Annika - Nika Cuisine
Ras Nigel Endell - Caribbean St Food
All the artists
All the Poetry4Grenfell and Dance4Grenfell Performing team including:
Lee Mya, Blacbird, Harriet Gore, Yinka a.k.a. Reason, Aamasade, Jaqi
Loye-Brown, Alexander D Great, Ricky Venel Stone and Kamau, Danjuma
Bihari, Kinetic Kizzita, EmpresS *1, Rebekah Raphael, Debbie 'Pan Diva'
Romain, Ras Makist, Debbie Golt, Human Jukebox and Rkayniine, Maya-
Louise, Chloe C, Elias and Daniella Chaffin, Akeera, Hayat, Eden-Rose,
Lion'el-Marcel-Raphael Jabbour, Zeena and Mrad, and Hemen, Rachel
and Naomi, Rabaab, KPA Dance Crew and Amen.
Kamitan Arts Foundation and CIC Trustees : Mrs Amal Jabbour, Mahlet R,
Annika Clinkett, Ricky Venel Stone and Shirine Osseiran.
I couldn't have done it without you, all of you, thank you! Dua!
Ankh-Wdja-Snb Amen Ashe'...

Art / Photo Credits

Artist Credits and Descriptions

All pictures taken by Emmanuelle Marcel 'Ja'bbour or Igor Barcelos for © Kamitan Arts except where stated below for art work or photos (in instances where art work is in background © is to the artist yet photo as a whole © Kamitan Arts):

Andrew Cooper, Marcia Robinson, Livingston Haynes, Stephanie Turner, JP and the rest of the Maxillla Wall of Truth artists - pgs.20, 66, 76, 88, 151, 175, 220

Andrew Wright - 'Eyesaw' - pg.116

Antony Marcano - pg.101

Braulio Barcelos - The Kamitan Arts logo of 'Ma'at', drawn and Acrylic paint for Kamitan Arts - pg.204

Book Launch and One Year On Show at the Bush Theatre, July 2018 - pg.156 and 203

Emmanuelle Marcel 'Ja' – Princess Emmanuelle words of 'Primeval Waters' written on heart - pg.100

Golden Heart Trellick Award won for "Poetry 4 Grenfell" 'Best Art Film' at Portobello Film Festival 2017 pg.195

Hesham Rahman's (RIP) Family - pg. 109

Isabella and Sophia - pg.105

Jaqi Loye-Brown photo of Grenfell Tower - pg.27

Junior Tomlin - pg.193

Karimah Dawoud - pgs.62, 79, 140

Laura Ann Hyland - 'From Syria to Grenfell' - pg.128

Lion'el-Marcel-Raphael Jabbour – pg.179

Mango and writers from CBM, West London Graff Crew - The Heart pg.54 and the 'Love for Grenfell' graffiti on the KPH - pg.84

Marina - 'Butterfly'- pg.63

Maya-Louise - pg. 173

Miranda 'Jar Lady' - Taken at Aesthesiarts' "Life-Blood Activism & Art" exhibition part of the Bloomsbury Festival, October 2018 - pg.127

Monera Takla – words of 'Beside the Fallen Ashes' written on heart - pg.100

Morpeth School children in Kamitan Arts Grenfell workshop - pg. 110

Pauline Antram - Dove sculpture - pg.172

Rachel Moidart - pg. 39

Thank you to all the little children that drew the beautiful chapter titles for us! Sophia and Isabella, Akeera, Zeena and Mrad, Hemen, Gisele and Adam, Yara, Lion'el-Marcel-Raphael. To all the children that took part in the workshops, including those photographed in the book: Sophia G, Tala, Ella, Liliy, Jessica, Julian, Merai and Eliora.

Andrew Cooper, Marcia Robinson and Livingston Haynes – Maxilla Wall of Truth

Banner - Andrew Cooper made with Livingstone Haynes, Marcia Robinson and input from the local community for the Wall of Truth. The design for this banner emerged initially from the painting I made on the concrete pillar in Maxilla Wall of Truth Area. I then later worked it into a drawing on the banner material and responded to people's suggestions. Livingstone said it was important to show children. He worked with me on the lettering and wording and Marcia added the hearts. This banner was mostly painted last winter (2017) in the Wall of Truth Area where Livingstone looks after it. "Using my artwork in this context means the stories as to how it's formed are an important part of the work" Andrew Cooper. www.andrewcooper-unseen.org

Marcia Robinson – Just solutions: infojustsolutions123@yahoo.co.uk
@Just Solutions123

Contact for the Wall Of Truth - maxwalloftruth@gmail.com
Facebook: Wall of Truth Maxilla Space

Junior Tomlin

A Founder member of the London cartoon workshop, Junior Tomlin has worked for various comic companies such as John Brown Jr. Publishing, Titan and Marvel comics. He worked as a digital colourist, credits include: Action Man, Transformers, Spiderman, Ninja Turtles, and Judge Dredd. He is also a educator and percussionist. His work on films include "Nightbreed", Lost in space and Ultra Guardians where he worked as a character designer and concept artist. He has also worked for Audio Rom, Saddlers Wells Theatre, IBT and many others.
The Grenfell Anniversary piece is my representation of all those who lost their lives in the fire and the hopes of the survivors to find peace justice and closure, which is overseen by angels.
www.retoxmagazine.com/art/junior-tomlin-the-salvador-dali-of-rave
www.fantazia.org.uk/Scene/players/juniortomlin.htm
www.juniortomlin.com/ www.imdb.com/name/nm3879892/
www.britishcomics.wikia.com/wiki/Junior_Tomlin
www.urbandandylondon.com/tag/junior-tomlin/

Shirine Osseiran - Colourtrail

olourtrail is a visual Art platform for creativity and expression. Founded by local Artist Shirine Osseiran in 2016 it delivers Art workshops for Children and Adults. Colourtrail's vision is to reconnect to the creative self inside each of us and to use the creative power of Colours to heal, inspire and empower our human spirit.
The A6 project Exhibition in January 2018 featured the work of 13 families who responded to the invite to do a daily drawing for one week. The drawings were exhibited along a year long project by Shirine and her daughter Hayat 8 years old at Acava Maxilla Studios (formerly the Maxilla Children's Centre).
www.colourtrail.com   www.shiroshiro.net info@colourtrail.com

Andrew Wright

Andrew Wright is an award winning urban artist who is exhibiting a new collection entitled "What I saw, what I see" at NuDawn, E9.

This intriguing and thought provoking collection aims to challenge complacency and is inspired by Wright's unique perception of the world around us. Much of Andrew's early work was heavily influenced by Reggae Hip Hop & Drum & Bass but whilst his works have been massively influenced by musicAndrew also desires to raise awareness of controversial issues surrounding race, youth culture and discrimination.

Andrew has the ability to approach sensitive subjects in a thought-provoking and original way. He seeks to invoke emotion in the viewer. Andrew produces diverse and unique works using a variety of mediums and techniques, recently working with stencils to produce a mural also digital art for books and websites. His style of work could be described as figurative, vibrant and colorful. He has conducted workshops and is passionate about sharing his skills and enthusiasm for art.

www.nudawn.london www.nineoarts.com www.artpardna.co.uk

Karimah Cuisina "the faith based well-being organisation"
Health & Well Being Representative for Charities in The Royal Borough of Kensington & Chelsea 2018
www.facebook.com/karimh.dawoud www.karimahscuisina.com @1karimah

From top (clockwise)
Kamitan Arts Workshop at Octavia
The Reed Centre, Ladbroke
Grove; EmpresS *1 with Jazzie B
and Igor 4Real at Acklam Village;
Dance4Grenfell at NK
Community Youth Festival;
Grace4Grenfell at Tabernacle; Live
on stage at the
Portobello Festival

From top (clockwise)
Poetry4Grenfell Team at Bush
Theatre One Year On Show; Soul
II Soul Charlotte Kelly Ft.
EmpresS *1@ Bush Theatre;
Chloe C and co - Poetry4Grenfell
at Kensington Primary Academy;
Hesham Rahman RIP's Nephew
Omar - 1st book given by
Lion'el-Marcel-Raphael Jabbour

Kamitan Arts & Friends

Ma'at, Ancient Kamitan (Egyptian) Deity of Justice and Truth, represents
order, right action and balance. May Ma'at bring about Justice and Truth
to the Grenfell Tower tragedy and to it's bereaved families.

Kamitan Arts CIC is a Non-Profit Community Company whose presence in the RBKC community has been evident for over 15 years. We work with children, young people and adults that are from disadvantaged backgrounds and challenging situations. Our objectives are to explore cultural identity and the heritage of our diverse community, as well as highlighting injustices and empowering women. We do this by promoting community cohesion and understanding of humanitarian issues through the performing arts. This includes workshops and productions in rap poetry, dance, drama, music, and film. All our programmes are inclusive and we always observe, critique and evaluate the learning and apply this to future work. Our work has taken us to Brazil, Egypt, Europe and Sudan. Kamitan Arts works with many artists and youth practitioners from Kensington and Chelsea, thus we're well-connected with the local voluntary and community sector.

For more information please contact:
ka.1@hotmail.co.uk @KamitanArts www.KamitanArts.com
www.twitter.com/KamitanArts www.fb.com/Poetry4Grenfell

"The immediate, tangible benefits of these workshops, as well as memorialising the voices of our young people are unquestionable and a vital part of this healing process. Community Relief supports Kamitan Arts to facilitate the continuation of this meaningful work."
Neleswa McLean-Thorne, Community Relief Project Coordinator (Oct 2017)
"Lovely to see the smiles returning to local people's faces after the Grenfell disaster.
Many thanks to Emmanuelle Marcel and Poetry4Grenfell"
Jonathan Barnett, Director of Portobello Film Festival - Song For Notting Dale neighbourhood party at the Maxilla Social Club (Aug 2017)
"Poetry 4 Grenfell" short later went on to be awarded PFF 2017's "Best Art Film"
"We were excited when Kamitan Arts brought "Poetry for Grenfell " to the Kids On the Green Cabaret, their performances were electric and had the audience captivated and deeply moved"
Zoe LeVack, Director of Kids on the Green (Nov 2017)

http://www.soulcentralmagazine.com/poetry4grenfell-gold-heart-trellick-film-nomination/
https://www.grenfellconnect.org.uk/directory/894/poetry-4-grenfell/
https://grenfellsupport.org/support/grenfell-projects/99
http://www.portobellofilmfestival.com/
https://www.spacehive.com/poetry-4-grenfell---voices-from-da-grove
https://www.bushtheatre.co.uk/event/poetry-4-grenfell/

MT Ink and its imprint Portobello Novella

Independent west London-based publishers creating contemporary biopgraphy and fiction, who acted as publishing consultants for the Poetry 4 Grenfell project. www.MT-Ink.co.uk

The Poetry4Grenfell Adults Team:

Aamasade

Shamanic Celebrant & Naturopathic Guide, Creative Facilitator & Poet, Djembe Percussionist~~
My service is to 'Realign and Instil the Values of Spiritual Harmony'. I offer this in a grounded language that is traditionally perfect for the moment. Ceremonies, Nature Events, Performance, Workshops, Rituals & Talks. I

co-create and facilitate organically with others where my objective always is to raise the vibration of our global village. I am available for ceremony presentations, Energy Balancing & Re-Alignment Sessions and have various energy balancing products available.

The name Aamasade means 'The Crowned Tree of Life' My message is that we are more connected than we are different... Blissfully Yours, AamaSade Shepnekhi.

Tree Circle Ceremonies "for all the cycles of life"

www.treecircleceremonies.co.uk

Alexander D Great

Born in Belmont, Port of Spain, on the beautiful island of Trinidad, Alexander D Great, aka D M Alexander Loewenthal [BA (hons)], moved to the UK at the age of four. He began his musical career aged 15 singing folk songs in London pubs and clubs. After a 30 – year career playing a variety of genres including Soul, Blues, R&B and Reggae, he returned to his calypso roots in the late 1980s, creating his own fusion of Calypso and Poetry, "Socablues". He is a classically trained musician, a poet, composer, writer, broadcaster, educator, and one of the UKs most accomplished Calypsonians.

• Twice winner of the Calypso Monarch title at London's Notting Hill Carnival

• Two years as Composer in Education for Performing Rights Society

• Tutor of Song writing at Rockschool, Selhurst College (later to become the BRITSCHOOL),

• Editorial consultant on Making Music – The Guide to Writing, Performing and Recording by George Martin

www.alexanderdgreat.net FB: @AlexanderDGreat Twitter: @AdGreat7

Yinka a.k.a. Reason EHFAR

Reason has been Rapping since 1988 and has worked with various Artists around the world. Such as Mc Mello, BrOTHERHOOD, Johnie D and Mista Stixx, Cash Crew, Chapter n Verse, Mark Morrison, Positive Beat, Rhtymn Within, Anita Baker, Black Moon USA Rappers, L.C.G. and has toured around the world. Reason is now back and Collaberating with A.W.O.L Collaberation (Reason,Johnie D,Mista Stixx,Mono Chorus)

FB.com/YinkaakaReason.EHFAR

Jaqi Loye-Brown

Jaqi Loye-Brown lives in west London, five minutes from Portobello Road and its vintage markets and eclectic demographic, an endless source of inspiration. Although with the Notting Hill area rapidly losing its boho charm, JLB indulges in reminiscing over halcyon times.

She describes herself as "a megalomaniac", home-schooled in guerrilla tactic creativity - music, spoken word, all matters digital & social, interior design, arts & crafts, influences her writing style. www.PortobelloNovella.com www.Facebook.com/JaqiLoyeBrownAuthor @PortoNovella

EmpresS *1 a.k.a. Princess Emmanuelle

International and Bi-lingual Rap-Poetess of Kamitan (Egyptian) heritage, Recording and touring artist of the Word, Sound 'n Power, as well as tutor in this discipline. Originally from Ladbroke Grove.

"Egypt's Sole Female Rapper" Egypt Today (Feb 2010)

@EmpresS1Egypt (FB, Twitter, Youtube)

www.soundcloud.com/empress1egypt

www.princessemmanuelle.bandcamp.com

www.reverbnation.com/EmpresS1

Harriet Gore - Touch Love Worldwide

Harriet Gore is a performing philosopher who lives and works in London where she has been a practising barrister in independent practice since 1997. Harriet has been involved in cases involving the application of Human Rights law including immigration and homelessness as well as other areas such as mental health and family law. Harriet is the founder of the worldwide movement -Touch LOVE Worldwide - and the leader and founding member of the LOVEtical (political) party Touch LOVE Worldwide (UK) which highlights the fact that LOVE is as fundamental as food and is a need which must be place at the centre of all decision making and actions.

www.touchloveworldwide.com

Shaun Clarke

Shaun aka VenomouStings and TheLifeSkool has been involved with rap and poetry spanning 2 decades, writing and performing, networking. He has written short stories and novels and hosted Benjamin Zephaniah in Leeds.

Since moving to Bristol he has been published on various platforms including Freedom of Mind and Bristol Cable, and interviewed by B24/7, and appeared live on Ujima CIC Radio and other platforms. Now (as part of Urban Word Collective) he compiles Lyrically Justified diverse poetry anthologies and curates Speaks Volumes showcases.
www.facebook.com/lifeskoolwriting/Lyricallyjustified.co.uk.

Poppy Seed

Poppy Seed is a performance poetry act that delivers a concept of conscious poetry and live music that educates, entertains and
inspires. It has been described as being "on the cusp of poetry and song. Poppy Seed is committed to Human Rights using her art to highlight Social justice campaigns; and to celebrate cultural diversity. In this light her eloquent activism has 'won' her title 'Warm Revolutionary.'
www.Poppyseedmusic.com
www.linkedin.com/in/angea-harvey-83302720

Lyrical Healer a.k.a. Winsome Duncan

Published poet and Book Confidence Coach. Winsome has over 20 years writing experience and enjoys living in her creative passion daily. As a songwriter she co-wrote the theme song 'Inside Out' which appears in the feature film, Moral Conflict which stars Mica Paris and Linda Robson. Her debut written song, 'Night Skies,' was recorded at the famous Bob Marley's Tuff Gong Studio, in Jamaica.Under the banner of her Lyrical Healer persona, she is a Performance Poet, Singer, Host, Journalist, Workshop Facilitator and has worked as a Radio Presenter. Lyrical has performed in a variety of prestigious venues like the Houses of Parliament, ITV Studios, Arsenal Emirates, The Royal festival Hall and Jazz café. Author of her second book An Inner City Guide to Surviving The Credit Crunch published by The Healing Factory. www.PeachesPublications.co.uk

Justice4Grenfell

Justice4Grenfell (J4G) is a community-led organisation, focused on the long term goal of obtaining justice for the bereaved families, survivors, evacuated residents and the wider local community, partnering with representative organisations. J4G will be engaging with the Public Inquiry. J4G was set up a few days after the Grenfell Fire disaster and officially launched on June 19th 2017 with the first of monthly silent walks – now held on the 14th of each month from Kensington Town Hall to the Grenfell Memorial Wall.

Together with many other local groups and individuals, J4G stepped into the void left by the authorities, to try to meet the urgent needs of those impacted. This work continues because of the on-going failure of the authorities to respond adequately to the disaster. Yvette Williams and Moyra Samuels, two strong women that are key to this movement. www.justice4grenfell.org justice4grenfell@gmail.com @officialJ4G

Grenfell United

Grenfell United is made up of the survivors and bereaved from the Grenfell Tower fire. Working together to provide as a strong, unified, independent and dignified voice for all those who survived or lost loved ones in the fire. We work to honour the memory of loved-ones who we lost and help rebuild the lives of the bereaved, survivors and the wider community. We campaign for truth and justice, and for change so that this never happens again. www.Grenfellunited.org @GrenfellUnited

Humanity for Grenfell

To ensure Truth, Justice, Restitution for all bereaved relatives and survivors of the Grenfell Tower fire and the local and wider effected community. Clarrie Mendy is the founder of Humanity for Grenfell which was set up immediately after the fire, where she lost her sister, Mary Mendy and niece, Khadija Saye (RIP). FB: @HumanityForGrenfell Twitter: @GrenfellHMNTY

The Grenfell Tower Community Monitoring Project

Is a community-led research project, run by the community for the community. It was set up in response to horrific Grenfell Tower fire tragedy, where many innocent lives were sadly lost.

The project monitors the support services that the Council provide in response to the Grenfell Tower Fire disaster. Our overarching aim is to safeguard the well-being of our community, now and in the future, by identifying where these services are falling short of what we need, and getting the Council to put it right. www.grenfellcommunitymonitoringproject.com grenfellmonitoringproject@gmail.com

Green for Grenfell - Toby Laurent Benson

The Green for Grenfell hashtag was started by local schools as they encouraged their students and others to raise awareness and generate donations for those affected by the Grenfell Tower fire. Since then, Green for Grenfell has been used to bring love, solidarity and remembrance in a variety of creative ways, from green clothes to green buildings to green Silent Walks. It is hoped that the community can continue to bring comfort to itself and others with a colour that signifies growth, resilience and balance. www.facebook.com/GreenForGrenfellOfficial/ @GreenForGrenfellOfficial

Community Relief Day

We provide: Acupuncture Guided meditation Poetry workshops Arts and crafts Science play Face painting and more... We hope through our activities, to in some small way facilitate the release of some of the pressure from our heavy hearts. FB: Community Relief Day

EPIC CIC

We deliver a range of youth support services to children and young people to help break down barriers so they can have the best life chances possible. www.Epiccic.org.uk @EPICCIC

Youth Action Alliance

The charity continues to work across North Kensington and its surrounding areas to deliver street-based and project work for young people, aged between 11 – 19 years old (up to 25 in certain circumstances). In addition, the charity works with a number of young adults, over the age of 18, who need support with employment, education or training. The remit, as stated in the YAA objectives, is to provide a variety of means to enhance young people's lives so that they are able to function in a changing economic climate.
www.Youthactionalliance.org

Westway 23

Westway23 was born as a consequence of the Trust's dubious 'Destination Westway' strategy. Many members of the local community were unhappy with the decisions being made to satisfy that strategy. Through a period of open meetings, discussion and in-depth research, it was concluded that now was the time to take a closer and sustained look at the Trust and the twenty-three acres of community land.

Commonly known as the 'Westway', the A40(M) elevated motorway was built between 1964 and 1970. Its construction was contro versial, as it caused huge destruction to a tightly-knit community and was essentially a failed experiment in alleviating congestion with an elevated ring-road around the entire of London. Through its construction a stretch of 23-acres of derelict land was created beneath it.

There is a community that has suffered the damage of such an enormous construction project and continues to suffer the deadly effects of poor air quality and noise pollution. Indeed, the effects on the people is one of the reasons the Ringways scheme was abandoned!

Through the direct actions of the local community in the 1960's the twenty-three acres were given to the local people as compensation for their continued suffering...
www.westway23.org/

24Hearts

24Hearts was started as a heartfelt and instinctive response to the tragedy at Grenfell Tower, with the aim of spreading love and representing the support and unity of the local community. The original idea was to create 24 hearts for the 24 floors in the tower, but the idea soon spread with local people coming together to create over 500 hearts. Thanks to all the brilliant heArtists who brought so much creativity to Maxilla Gardens over the summer of 2017.
www.24hearts.org/

Latimer Community Art Therapy Trust

Art Therapy is a psychological therapy involving both verbal comm-unication and communication through art and play. The sessions provide a private, non-judgmental space in which children, adolescents and adults can express and process their feelings and experiences. The use of art to contain the things so hard to make sense of has been fundamental to the community throughout. All the Art Psychotherapists are fully qualified at MA level, HCPC registered and DBS vetted. The therapy team are now well known to the community and provide consistent, contained ongoing support. The first space was at Henry Dickens Estate and the work expanded to local primary schools, nurseries, adult services and four other community hubs. Through the help of funders Thomas's School Foundation, The Teapot Trust, Vout-O-Renees gallery and children's services the art therapy services will continue long term in the community. Sessions can be accessed by drop in or individual work can be set up as needed within the community spaces. www.lcat.org.uk/

Henry Dickens

The Henry Dickens (HD) Junior Club evolved from the art therapy service at Henry Dickens where children began to need different support in the months following the fire. The club provides creative, educational and physical activities from 3.15 – 5.30pm on Monday, Tuesday and Friday and from 12 – 3pm on a Saturday.

The HD Junior club is staffed by qualified teaching assistants, teachers and experienced youth workers. The provision is structured around providing a safe space where children can learn new skills and experiment with different activities; get active outdoors with an experienced games coach and participate in cooking.
http://lcat.org.uk.gridhosted.co.uk/henry-dickens/

Grenfell Hope Project

Grenfell Hope Project is a large group of volunteers committed to building a resilient community following the fire disaster that happened on 14th of June, 2017 in West London. We will not replicate any work but rather fill in the gaps in disaster response, relief and recovery as the efforts continue. We provide basic psychosocial training to the volunteers who will be working in the area. We also provide trainers' training and Workers' Support. We hope to create free arts, sports, drama, yoga, playtherapy programs for the children who live near the Grenfell Tower. These programs are expected to last at least six months. The aim is to facilitate and promote the natural resilience within individuals, families and communities.
Grenfellhopeproject@gmail.com

Angels 4 Grenfell

Angels4Grenfell is a resident-led initiative inspired by the strength, resilience and skilled of the diverse community in Notting Dale- they are our true asset.
www.angels4grenfell.com hope@angels4grenfell.org

OREMI Centre

Mental health day centre offering outreach, advice and information and community development. Since the Grenfell fire, OREMI has reached out into the community to support survivors and the bereaved.
malcolm.phillips@hestia.org

Grenfell Tower Inquiry

The Grenfell Tower Inquiry is an independent public inquiry, set up to examine the circumstances leading up to and surrounding the fire at Grenfell Tower on 14 June 2017. It was ordered by Prime Minister Theresa May on the following day.
www.Grenfelltowerinquiry.org.uk

Grenfell Support

@RBKC provides information and support to people affected by the tragedy at #GrenfellTower Account monitored 9am-5pm, Mon-Fri
www.Grenfellsupport.org.uk   @GrenfellSupport

Grenfell Connect

Grenfell Connect is a volunteer-run, unaffiliated website which was set up in summer 2017 in the aftermath of the devastating fire on 14 June 2017, with the aim be a central information touchpoint for the community affected by the Grenfell Tower fire. We collated and shared information about organisations, events and meetings set up to help the communities in and around North Kensington.
www.Grenfellconnect.org

Grenfell Voices

A charity CIC to support and facilitate creative work of survivors, bereaved and first responders of the Grenfell Tower fire, by connecting them with industry professionals in film, music & art to realise their vision and amplify their voices. We launched at the Electric Cinema on December 13th 2017 and have been featured in national press, radio and TV, including features by Jon Snow on Channel 4 News and BBC Newsnight. Grenfell Voices is the Artists for Justice for Grenfell Group. info@grenfellvoices.com
www.se1productions.com/grenfellvoices/   @GrenfellVoices

Kids On the Green

Kids on the Green opened in the wake of the Grenfell Tower disaster to provide a safe space for local children, teens and families. We offer our local community free arts and crafts, sports, refreshments and a whole host of other weird and wonderful activities - circus skills, pottery, homeopathy and hair braiding to name just a few. Our team of qualified child and family therapists ensure that the emotional well being of our families is prioritised. @KOTG @KidsonthegreenW11

Off Road Circus

Off Road Circus Project is a social circus with the aim to provide relief through play, circus and theatre activities to children of marginalised communities or those affected by disaster. Off Road Circus was the first Circus Project to respond to the aftermath of the Grenfell Tower Fire. Alongside Kids on the Green, Off Road Circus Project delivers free workshops available to the children of Grenfell and the affected community and will continue to do so for many months to come. @realamyg @offroadcircusproject

Fer Arts

Fer Arts is an artist led non-profit arts organisation, curating collaborative exhibitions, developing community projects and supporting emerging creatives and artist management at 0% commission. We promote urban art and photography from artists influenced by UK street culture through innovative concept shows and platforming creatives.
18-30. www.ferarts.org @ferarts

Grace 4 Grenfell

Gospel music concerts and projects that embrace all sorts of musical disciplines and artists from the community, strengthening one another through music post-Grenfell, led by a survivor.
@Grace4Grenfell

Echo Sourcing

Echo Sourcing are a design-to-delivery garment supplier working with major fashion retailers across Europe since 1996. Echo are based in the UK, Turkey and Bangladesh and remain one of the leading companies in terms of ethical trading and sourcing in their field. 'Ninety Percent' is a charitable fashion line run by Echo wherein 90% of profits from sales are donated to the buyers choice of causes supported by the company such as The Childrens Hope charity, War Child UK, Wild Aid and Big Life Foundation. Echo Sourcing donated 60 Poetry 4 Grenfell T-Shirts.

Reclamation

Reclamation is an emerging initiative which focuses on empowerment through literature and the arts founded in response to the Grenfell fire. By utilising creativity as a means for social commentary and emotional growth we believe it is possible to begin healing both individual and historical traumas. The name Reclamation comes from this idea of reclaiming identity and autonomy through creative expression and exposure. Reclamation currently procures funding and support for existing arts projects and workshops in West London.

Zita Holbourne

Co-founder / National Chair BARAC UK
Poet, Writer, Artist, Curator
www.blackactivistsrisingagainstcuts.blogspot.com
www.zitaholbourne.com

Karnak House

Karnak House was incarnated in 1975 as Caribbean Cultural International, an organization of writers and artists coming together to create a new platform for the work of Caribbean and Black British writers and artists in Britain. The work was directed to art exhibitions (including photography), poetry readings and lectures.

Because of the nature of London, CCI decided to embrace the African community and changed its name to Karnak House, with its base on Westbourne Park Road, Notting Hill, since 1977.

Our first book, New Planet, was an anthology of new and previously published poetry and mixed the older generation, John La Rose & Kamau Brathwaite, Marc Matthews with the younger. National and international recognition came with the publication of I is a Long-memoried woman by Grace Nichols, which won the Commonwealth Poetry Prize 1983. It also won the Guyana Poetry Prize, followed by Marc Matthews winning the same prize for our publication of his first book, Guyana My Altar. In 1985 Karnak House published Amon Saba Saakana's first published novel, Blues Dance, which received national attention and a phone call from Faber & Faber's then chairman. Karnak House sets out to realize two objectives: to continuously locate and publish books by Caribbean and African writers in the field of creative fiction and poetry. Works that innovate and call into being new ways of presenting material from the unflinching perspectives of the working class, primarily. The second objective and front is to renew and reinterpret African civilizations through the prism of Africans themselves or progressive writers of any ethnic background. The works of Cheikh Anta Diop, Théophile Obenga, Jacob Carruthers and Charles S. Finch are the best examples in this category. We believe that our contribution to publishing in Britain has shaped and influenced mainstream British publishers in the aesthetic way in which they now present African and Caribbean material; the design and visual presentation of books, and the emphasis now on the young British-born writers and artists.

Our publications set the benchmark for others to follow and we are not afraid of controversy and the demolition of European colonial literary and historical orthodoxy. www.karnakhouse.co.uk

Nika's Kitchen

@NikasKitchen www.nikaskitchen.com nikaskitchen@gmail.com

Love Gift Vegan

Prosperityandlove7@gmail.com
www.Lovegiftvegan.co.uk

Caribbean Street Food
@CaribbeanStFood

About The Author

Princess Emmanuelle a.k.a. EmpresS *1

Emmanuelle Marcel 'Ja'bbour, the Founding Director of Kamitan Arts, is a British female bi-lingual Rap-Poetess, Humanitarian, Choreographer and Freelance Performing Arts facilitator of Afrikan and Middle Eastern heritage, that is very fond of her Sa3ayda, Upper Egyptian roots. A professionally trained Dancer (RTS, NSCD, BRIT,Urdang, LCDS), that used the Spoken Word to channel her artistic expression and emotionally heal after a serious dance injury nearly two decades ago. In the early 2000's she entered the Spoken Word profession as 'Princess Emmanuelle' and hasn't looked back since, having her work published in newspapers, magazines, books, albums and aired on radio and TV internationally. Princess Emmanuelle deliver Dance and Rap-Poetry workshops, working on performances, and collaborating on productions fusing Dance, Drama, and Poetry through Hip-Hop -Theatre with her community company Kamitan Arts (KA).

" EmpresS *1 is holding the flag for women who are generally under-represented in the arts and cultural world, specifically in the Hip-Hop scene. THE 'First Female Egyptian Rapper' has the guts to address those MAJOR issues such as Freedom of Speech, Women's Rights etc and manages to be extremely respected for that, all over the Egyptian media, because her music talks about Love, Justice, Equality, Freedom, Respect, Unity, Dual Identity, Oppression, Peace, Female Independence..." (Afrolution.com 2011)

"Egypt's Sole Female Rapper" Egypt Today (Feb 2010) has toured the UK, Egypt, Brazil, Sudan, Berlin, Lebanon performing her Rap-Poetry and Reggae and running workshops in different dance styles, drama and Rap-Poetry (Word Sound 'n Power) for 15 years. She started off as a Poetess in 1999 as Princess Emmanuelle, although was writing since the age of 7, many moonlights before. It wasShaun Clarke (Mr Kick -Mad Move UK) that initiated her with the name Empress at the time she was preparing to release her first Spoken Word album "Born Into a Drowning World" in 2001/2, this name later developed into EmpresS *1. Notably EmpresS *1 has shared stages and opened up for some greats such as Jocelyn Brown (UK), PUBLIC ENEMY (UK/US), Gyptian (UK/JA), West el Balad (Egypt), O Rappa (Aracaju, Brazil), Raconais MCs (with Julio Serrano in Rio, Brazil), Dawn Penn (UK), Keith Murray (UK/US) and Al Griffiths from The Gladiators (Brazil/JA), Suheir Hammad (UK/US), Benjamin Zephaniah (Birmingham and Egypt), and has taught Rap-Poetry and Dance in the favelas of Rio de Janeiro and Bahia in Brazil and more elaborate prestigious places such as the Royal Opera House for Walid Aouni's Contemporary Dance Company.

Princess Emmanuelle's TV, Radio and Magazine credits include: ESC, Ch 2 Egypt ("Sabah el Kher ya Misr" - Good Morning Egypt), BBC, BEN TV, ITV, Nile TV, OTV, Aperipê TV and Radio, The Voice, New Nation, Kensington and Chelsea Times, On Route, Spirit, Community Times, Egypt Today, Wash Washa, Marie Claire Italy, I Am Hip-Hop Magazine, So3t el Arab Radio, Genesis FM, Life FM, Rhythm FM, Resonance FM, Omega FM, Horytna Radio, BBC World.

Most recently Princess Emmanuelle's poetry has been published in Arkbound's "Lyrically Justified" compiled by Urban Word Collective and is heralded as the "Streetwise Bible" and her Spoken Word released on the Eardrum's 'Colonised' album, a track entitled "Iya el Donia" (Mother of the World in Egyptian and Yoruba), receiving a great Songlines review!

Artistic Director and Founder of Kamitan Arts CIC, the Director of the award-winning film "Poetry 4 Grenfell" (Portobello Film Festival's 'Best Art film' 2017), and the compiler and editor of this 'Poetry 4 Grenfell Voices from da Grove and Latimer' book, Princess Emmanuelle's "Poetry 4 Grenfell" project manifested as an immediate response to help artistically deal with the emotional aftermath of the Grenfell fire in June 2017. Kamitan Arts has been offering voluntary Rap-Poetry and Dance workshops to those affected, to help them address their emotions and begin to heal.

Princess Emmanuelle is a life-long resident of Ladbroke Grove, and naturally this project and book is something that is very close to her heart
.

www.fb.com/Poetry4Grenfell
www.fb.com/Empres1Egypt
www.KamitanArts.com

ЄЖ3

@KamitanArts   @Poetry4Grenfell   @EmpresS1Egypt

"...Beautiful London poet Emmanuelle, of African and Arabian heritage, talented, prolific and passionate about her art, she has chosen to express herself through metaphor, meter and rhyme."
(The Voice, Feb 23, 2003)

"'I know that poetry is the way forward,' she says with the conviction of a priestess and the twang of a West London teenager."
(The Voice, Feb 23, 2003)

"A lot of thought-provoking, positive lyrics that touch on almost every aspect off human endeavours are all included in 'Born Into a Drowning World'...At nineteen, age has imprinted her name boldly in the sand of history" (The African Voice, Jan 2003)

"Emmanuelle is a vision in colour..Upon meeting her you can tell immediately that she is a force to be reckoned with." (Community Times, Feb 2008)

"With a name like Princess Emmanuelle there comes a lot of questions and a lot of expectations..I only hoped that the Princess did not disappoint....and she did not." (Community Times, Feb 2008)

"Princess Emmanuelle aw EmpresS *1 aw bel A3rabi 'El Embradora al 2oola' (الامبراطورة الاولى), mesh bas sha3era, raqesa, mosamema, we momasela, ...di Awel Bent Rapper fi Misr!..."
("Sabah el Kher Ya Misr", on ESC and Egyptian Ch2,
Wed 17th March 2010)